AAT

Level 4

Diploma in Professional Accounting

Internal Accounting Systems and Control

Course Book

For assessments from September 2024

 **BPP**

First edition 2021

Third edition 2024

ISBN 9781035516377

Previous ISBN 9781035505951

ISBN (for internal use only) 9781035516216

Previous ISBN (for internal use only) 9781035504961

eISBN 9781035516728

British Library Cataloguing-in-Publication Data

A catalogue record for this book is available from the British Library

Published by

BPP Learning Media Ltd

BPP House, Aldine Place

142-144 Uxbridge Road

London W12 8AA

United Kingdom

learningmedia.bpp.com

Printed in the United Kingdom

> Your learning materials, published by BPP Learning Media Ltd, are printed on paper obtained from traceable sustainable sources.

A note about copyright

Contents

Introduction to the course

Syllabus overview

All organisations must guard against fraud through good control systems. However, many businesses underestimate both the probability and impact of employee fraud. Those working within the accounts department play a pivotal role in guarding against misuse of resources, and the key aim of this unit is to provide students with the tools to evaluate internal controls and to recommend improvements.

The unit teaches students to consider the role and responsibilities of the accounting function, including the needs of key stakeholders who use financial reports to make decisions. Students will review accounting systems to identify weaknesses and will make recommendations to mitigate identified weaknesses in future operations. Students will apply several analytical methods to evaluate the implications of any changes to operating procedures.

The structure of the accounting function, which varies depending on the size of the organisation, must comply with statutory requirements. Students will learn to identify appropriate controls, assess their impact in terms of cost-effectiveness, reliability and timeliness, and ensure that all functions adapt their working practices to meet new requirements in an ethical and sustainable way.

Technology is changing the way that accountancy information is processed, and this unit requires knowledge of the fundamental principles of data analytics and artificial intelligence (AI), which may be used as an alternative way to gather and analyse information. Cloud accounting is changing the way accountants work and visualisation, including dashboards, is increasingly used to present information in a way that is easier for stakeholders to understand. Data security and breaches are regularly reported in the press, and therefore it is imperative that students are aware of the importance of keeping all data secure and consider the confidential nature of the data that they will be processing as part of their everyday role.

Finally, students will evaluate the impact of changes on the system and its users, identifying different methods of support that can be given to users of the accounting system to assist them in adapting to the recommended improvements.

This unit has close links with:

* Level 3 Business Awareness
* Level 4 Applied Management Accounting
* Level 4 Audit and Assurance

Test specification for Internal Accounting Systems and Controls unit assessment

Assessment method	Marking type	Duration of assessment
Computer based assessment	Partially computer / partially human marked	2.5 hours

Learning outcomes	Weighting
1. Understand the role and responsibilities of the accounting function within an organisation	10%
2. Evaluate internal control systems	25%
3. Evaluate an organisation's accounting system and underpinning procedures	25%
4. Understand the impact of technology on accounting systems	15%
5. Recommend improvements to an organisation's accounting system	25%
Total	100%

Assessment structure

2½ hours duration.

Competency is 70%.

The total number of marks for this assessment is 100.

*Note that this is only a guideline as to what might come up, based on the AAT's Sample Assessments. The format and content of each task may vary from what we have listed below.

Your assessment will consist of five tasks.

The assessment will take the form of a computer-based test, which will include extended writing tasks. The assessment will require both computer and human marking and as such, the results will take approximately 6 weeks to be finalised and published.

Task	Expected content	Approx. marks (per sample)	Chapter reference	Study complete
Task 1	Purpose, structure and organisation of the accounting function. Type of question: picklist, ticks.	25	The accounting function Impact of technology	
Task 2	The types of fraud in the workplace combined with ways in which it can be prevented and/or detected. Type of question: picklist, ticks, written question.	25	Internal control systems Accounting systems	
Task 3	The effectiveness of internal controls. Type of question: picklist, ticks.	10	Internal control Systems Accounting systems	
Task 4	The monitoring of accounting systems and how they work in practice. Type of question: picklist, ticks, written question.	15	Accounting systems	
Task 5	The analysis of internal controls with recommendations to improve whilst considering the impact on users. Type of question: picklist, ticks, written question.	25	Impact of technology Making changes to systems	

Skills bank

Our experience of preparing students for this type of assessment suggests that to obtain competency, you will need to develop a number of key skills.

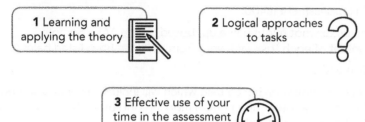

1 Learning and applying the theory

2 Logical approaches to tasks

3 Effective use of your time in the assessment

What do I need to know to do well in the assessment?

This unit is one of the mandatory Level 4 units. *Internal Accounting Systems and Controls* is a broad syllabus that is examined by a mixture of written questions as well as picklist, drag and drop, gapfill and true/false type questions.

To be successful in the assessment you need to:

• Understand the role and responsibilities of the accounting function within an organisation

• Evaluate internal control systems

• Evaluate an organisation's accounting system and underpinning procedures

• Understand the impact of technology on accounting systems

• Recommend improvements to an organisation's accounting system

Assumed knowledge

Internal Accounting Systems and Controls is a **mandatory** unit. In order to perform well in this unit we recommend that you ensure you are familiar with the following topics covered in your previous Level 3 *Business Awareness*, Level 4 *Applied Management Accounting* and Level 4 *Drafting and Interpreting Financial Statements* studies:

• Stakeholders

• Ethics

• Fraud

• Internal controls (SPAMSOAP)

• Management accounting reports

• Artificial Intelligence and machine learning, data analytics, cloud accounting

• Data visualisation

• PESTLE

• Legal and regulatory reports

• Accounting ratios

Assessment style

In the unit assessment you will complete tasks by:

(a) Entering narrative by selecting from drop-down menus of narrative options known as **picklists**

(b) Using **drag and drop** menus to enter narrative

(c) Typing in numbers, known as **gapfill** entry

(d) Entering **ticks**

(e) Entering **dates** by selecting from a calendar

(f) Entering extended **written answers** for human marking.

You must familiarise yourself with the style of the online questions and the AAT software before taking the unit assessment. As part of your revision, log in to the **AAT website** and attempt their **online practice assessments**.

Each question style is explained in more detail below.

Picklists

Here you need to answer questions by selecting the appropriate wording from a list of options. These options will be given in a drop down box and be presented in alphabetical order.

An example is given below taken from the AAT *Internal Accounting Systems and Controls Unit Assessment* Sample Assessment 1 Task 1 part (b):

(b)(ii) Identify the correct risk for each statement below.

Statement	Risk
You decide that to save time, you will leave your laptop in your car overnight. To ensure that it is safe, you will put it in the boot.	
You receive an email from a supplier's new email address that asks you to click on a link in order to access their new bank details.	
Grace, your office cleaner, has unplugged the main server in order to plug in her vacuum cleaner to clean the room.	
Hattie has decided to deactivate her antivirus software as it makes her PC too slow.	
You are rushing to send a quote to an existing customer and to save time do not look up the email address as you can remember it.	

Options
Unauthorised remote access
Phishing
Loss of data
Physical loss of equipment
Data issued in error

(5 marks)

Gapfill entry

You may be asked to calculate a specific number and then enter it into the proforma / solution box on-screen. This is known as gapfill entry.

Entering ticks

Several short-form objective style questions will require you to indicate your answer by entering a tick. For example:

- 'Yes' or 'no'
- 'True' or 'false'
- ticking to indicate your choice of number.

The following question appears in the AAT *Internal Accounting Systems and Controls Unit Assessment* Sample Assessment 1 Task 1 part (c):

(c)(ii) Identify whether the following statements about the advantages of using data analytics in accounts are true or false.

 BPP

Statement	True ✔	False ✔
Data analytics uses a variety of techniques such as critical thinking, logic and complex quantitative methods in order to create accurate future predictions.		
Data visualisation is relevant to all data analytics.		

(2 marks)

You may need to read the scenario and requirement several times in order to understand the requirement before you enter a tick in the correct box.

Extended writing skills

The Level 4 *Internal Accounting Systems and Control* Unit Assessment will be assessing **application** as well as knowledge. There will be a number of questions which require an extended written response. It is recommended that you follow these tips to support their learning for this assessment:

- Practise the questions in the *Internal Accounting Systems and Control* Question Bank and from within this Course Book.
- Analyse your answers against the sample answers given. Consider whether your answer is answering the given question, whether your response is specific to the given scenario and whether you can support your judgements using figures and information provided from the scenario.
- The AAT has useful question and style tips on their website, which can be found at: www.aat.org.uk/training/study-support/search. In particular, the 'Writing skills' and 'Unit assessment support' offer useful advice towards preparing your writing techniques for this assessment.
- Complete the practice assessments which will enable you to test your time management skills as well as practice your extended writing abilities.

The extended written answers may be short answers, requiring one or two sentences, such as this extract from Task 2 in the AAT *Internal Accounting Systems and Controls Unit Assessment* Sample Assessment 1 part (b):

(b)(i) Identify FOUR weaknesses in the system that mat result in fraud occurring.

(4 marks)

(b)(ii) Recommend an internal control for EACH weakness, giving a reason why it will help prevent fraud.

(8 marks)

Weakness that may result in fraud	Internal control to help prevent fraud and reason

In this case, the candidates are being asked for four weaknesses in the system that may result in fraud and to recommend an internal control (with a reason) which could prevent the fraud recurring. Here, there is one mark available for the identification of the weakness and a further two marks to recommend an internal control and explain why it would prevent the fraud recurring. Therefore, sufficient information must be written to explain the issue and why this may be the case, but there is no need to write an overly long explanation as the maximum points available are three marks per valid weakness.

Alternatively, the answer may require more detail, and a larger amount of space will be available to input your answer. Look carefully at the marking allocation to give an indication of the level of detail required.

Read the question carefully

The main verbs used for these type of question requirements are:

Identify – analyse and select for presentation

Explain – set out in detail the meaning of

Discuss – by argument, discuss the pros and cons

Step 1   READ the question carefully

It is important to read the question carefully to identify exactly what is being asked of you. It is a good idea to highlight key words and all verbs as this will ensure you answer the question that is being asked, not the question you think they should ask!

Step 2   PLAN your answer

Once you have established the requirement, note down what you know about the topic, **relevant** to what is being asked (key words only). It is a good idea to do this on a piece of paper so you can eliminate irrelevant knowledge and formulate a logical answer when you enter it on screen.

You must familiarise yourself with the style of the online questions and the AAT software before taking the assessment. As part of your revision, login to the **AAT website** and attempt their **online practice assessments**.

Introduction to the assessment

The question practice you do will prepare you for the format of tasks you will see in the AAT *Internal Accounting Systems and Controls* Unit Assessment.

Information on the scenario for your AAT *Internal Accounting Systems and Controls* Unit Assessment is issued in advance of the assessment as pre-seen material. You must make sure you are familiar with the relevant pre-seen material before sitting your assessment. The pre-seen scenario for the live assessment should be downloaded from the AAT website (www.aat.org.uk/training/study-support/search).

Note that the scenario is also included as a pop-up in the live assessment, but it is strongly advised that you familiarise yourself with the information prior to the assessment.

It is also useful to familiarise yourself with the other introductory information you **may** be given at the start of the assessment. The following is provided at the beginning of the sample unit assessment for illustration:

Assessment information

You have 2 hours and 30 minutes to complete this sample assessment.

- This assessment contains 5 tasks and you should attempt to complete every task,
- Each task is independent. You will not need to refer to your answers to previous tasks.
- The total number of marks for this assessment is 100.
- Read every task carefully to make sure you understand what is required.
- Where the date is relevant, it is given in the task data.
- Both minus signs and brackets can be used to indicate negative numbers unless task instructions state otherwise.
- You must use a full stop to indicate a decimal point. For example, write 100.57 not 100,57 or 10057.
- You may use a comma to indicate a number in the thousands, but you don't have to. For example, 10000 and 10,000 are both acceptable.

Scenario

The tasks in this assessment are all based on the scenario of Enabell Ltd.

You are Taylor Jones, an Accounting Technician working for Enabell Ltd.

The company has recently undergone a management buyout which has resulted in a new management team being brought in, including a new Managing Director (Sean Brown) and Operations Director (Paul Brown).

The new management team have asked you to review the internal controls and identify any weakness that need to be addressed.

Note. The **AAT sample assessment** (sometimes referred to as the **practice assessment**) uses a company called **Enabell Ltd** as part of the scenario and reference material. This is not the same organisation as the one used in the live assessment. At the time of publication, the organisation that will be used for the **live assessment** is called **Downton Instruments Ltd**.

(a) As you revise, use the **BPP Passcards** to consolidate your knowledge. They are a pocket-sized revision tool, perfect for packing in that last-minute revision.

(b) Attempt as many tasks as possible in the **Exam Practice Kit**. There are plenty of assessment-style tasks which are excellent preparation for the real unit assessment.

(c) Always **check** through your own answers as you will in the real unit assessment, before looking at the solutions in the back of the Exam Practice Kit.

Key to icons

Key term

A key definition which is important to be aware of for the assessment.

Formula to learn

A formula you will need to learn as it will not be provided in the assessment.

Formula provided

A formula which is provided within the assessment and generally available as a pop-up on screen.

Activity

An example which allows you to apply your knowledge to the technique covered in the Course Book. The solution is provided at the end of the chapter.

Illustration

A worked example which can be used to review and see how an assessment question could be answered.

Assessment focus point

A high priority point for the assessment.

Open book reference

Where use of an open book will be allowed for the assessment.

Real life examples

A practical real life scenario.

AAT qualifications

The material in this book may support the following AAT qualifications:

AAT Diploma in Professional Accounting Level 4 and AAT Diploma in Professional Accounting at SCQF Level 8.

Supplements

From time to time we may need to publish supplementary materials to one of our titles. This can be for a variety of reasons, from a small change in the AAT unit guidance to new legislation coming into effect between editions.

You should check our supplements page regularly for anything that may affect your learning materials. All supplements are available free of charge on our supplements page on our website at: learningmedia.bpp.com/pages/resources-for-students

Improving material and removing errors

BPP Learning Media do everything possible to ensure the material is accurate and up to date when sending to print. In the event that any errors are found after the print date, they are uploaded to the following website: learningmedia.bpp.com/pages/errata

These learning materials are based on the qualification specification released by the AAT in April 2024.

 BPP

1 The accounting function

Learning outcomes

1.1 The accounting function

Learners need to understand:

1.1.1 the importance of ethics and sustainability within the accounting function

1.1.2 the importance of accuracy and cost-effectiveness within the accounting system

1.1.3 why different types and sizes of organisation or departments within an organisation will require different accounting information and systems

1.1.4 the different accounting team staffing structures (centralised and decentralised) that will be required by different types or sizes of organisation:

- length of scalar chain
- levels of management
- span of control.

1.2 Financial information used by stakeholders

Learners need to understand:

1.2.1 different stakeholders of an organisation:

- internal
- external

1.2.2 the purpose of financial information produced for:

- internal use
- external use

1.2.3 how financial information is used by stakeholders

1.2.4 that financial information must comply with legislation and regulation

1.2.5 the importance of ethical information and sustainability practices to stakeholders

1.2.6 that stakeholders use the following types of financial reports:

- statement of profit or loss
- statement of changes in equity
- statement of financial position
- statement of cash flow
- budgetary control reports.

1.3 Changes to management information

Learners need to understand:

1.3.1 how organisational requirements will inform the management information system:

- size of organisation
- strategic goals
- legislation and regulation

1.3.2 how management information systems should enable the calculation of performance indicators:

- gross profit margin
- operating profit margin
- current ratio
- quick (acid test) ratio
- inventory turnover
- inventory holding period (days)
- trade receivables collection period
- trade payables collection period
- gearing
- return on capital employed (ROCE)

1.3.3 why changes may be required to existing systems to meet revised organisational requirements.

Assessment context

The topics covered in this chapter will be included within a number of tasks in the Internal Accounting Systems and Controls unit assessment.

Qualification context

Accounting regulations and the preparation of statutory financial statements have been covered in *Drafting and Interpreting Financial Statements* at Level 4. Different types of organisation and accounting regulations are covered at an introductory level in *Financial Accounting: Preparing Financial Statements* at Level 3.

Management accounting has been studied at Level 3 and also in *Applied Management Accounting* at Level 4.

Business context

All businesses have some form of accounting function, even if some or all of it is outsourced to external providers. How the accounting function is structured and run, and how it uses the accounting system, is of key importance to the company's success.

The culture of an accounting function will be dictated by the size of the organisation, but often the biggest influence is the management style, and this will have an impact of the level of internal controls implemented, the morale and efficiency of staff.

An accounting function must produce the required management information both accurately and on a timely basis. This information is used by the management team who can then make the necessary organisational decisions in order to ensure the business is run effectively.

Accountants need to understand the purpose of the internal and external reports they create, and how this information will be used by a variety of stakeholders. When preparing reports, you must consider why the information is required, so that it can be provided in the appropriate format and with the appropriate level of detail, bearing in mind the needs of the reader(s) of the report.

Chapter overview

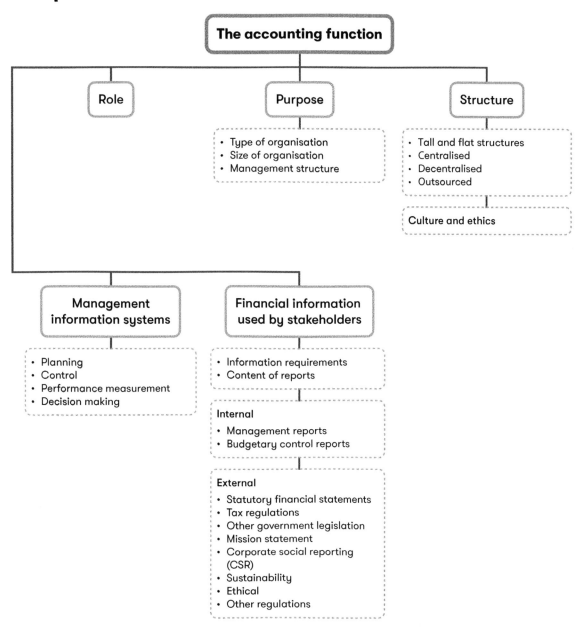

Introduction

In this chapter we look at the accounting function of an organisation and review different approaches to such functions in the context of structure.

Many organisations centralise functions such as accounting and even outsource all or some of the role of the accounting function to third parties. We will consider the impact this has on the organisation and its accounting function, and how they operate.

Organisations are heavily influenced by their **stakeholders** – individuals or groups who are in some way affected by the organisation's actions. Stakeholders can be categorised as either internal or external. Those running an organisation, and its accounting function, must consider the varying needs of its stakeholders when making decisions.

In this chapter, we evaluate the importance of the financial statements and how they are used by both internal and external stakeholders.

1 Role of the accounting function

The role of the accounting function is to provide information:

- To Groceries Supply Code of Practice (GSCOP) through both financial and management accounting information
- To external stakeholders through financial accounting information (published financial statements)

KEY
TERM

> **Management accounting:** Provides managers with financial information that they can use in order to make critical decisions that affect how the company is run.
>
> **Financial accounting:** Producing financial statements and other external reports for regulators, including taxation, about the position and performance of the company for a certain time period.

The accounting function should be set up to ensure that the information it produces is accurate and useful for both internal and external stakeholders. An organisation can ensure these objectives are met by establishing robust processes and controls. These will enable an organisation's employees to understand exactly what is required of them, and ensure that there is sufficient training, time and resources allocated, so that they can provide this information to the standard required.

2 Purpose and structure of the accounting function

2.1 Purpose of the accounting function

The purpose of the accounting function is:

- To process all accounting transactions for the company accurately and completely
- To provide information to stakeholders that is correct and up to date

2.2 Types of organisation

There are many different types of organisation. You need to be able to recognise why the type of organisation affects how it is structured and how it operates. In turn, these factors affect the accounting function, and the accounting and internal control systems, of the organisation.

2.2.1 Profit making organisations

Many organisations (eg companies) are set up to make a profit, so their main objective will be to achieve a level of profit that meets the expectations of the owners (shareholders, partners, sole trader). These organisations will want to know about the financial results and compare them against financial performance targets, eg actual costs against budgeted costs.

2.2.2 Not-for-profit organisations

Not-for-profit organisations exist to perform a service or support a group of people to achieve a variety of objectives. These organisations include:

- Charities
- Social enterprises (community interest companies)
- Sports clubs
- 'Friends' societies (arts, schools, hospitals)
- Mutual societies (credit unions)

External regulatory requirements will dictate to a certain degree how formalised the accounting function of such organisations will be; for example, a small local village hall fundraising club will have a treasurer and a committee, but no formalised financial function. A larger charity like Cancer Research UK will have the financial reporting infrastructure in place to support its external reporting functions and internal control requirements and to liaise with the various charity shops, online fundraising resources, outreach groups, and so forth.

2.3 Size of organisation

The size of the organisation will also affect what accounting information is required and what controls are in place to ensure accurate and timely information.

These factors also affect the specific tasks the accounting function performs.

A small organisation is likely to only have a small number of staff and staff within the accounting function may be organised to perform multiple tasks or controls which increases the risk of fraud within an organisation.

In larger accounting functions of big organisations, there may be clear sections of the function which perform the different tasks. In addition to both **financial** and **management accounting**, there may be separate sections for the following:

Transaction processing: Maintaining the accounting records: payroll, receivables ledger, payables ledger, cash book and general ledger.

Treasury management: Managing the organisation's cash flow and requirements for finance.

Activity 1: Multitasking in a small organisation

Activities in this unit are based on the CCC scenario (which can be found at the back of this Course Book).

At CCC, the staff often multitask. Although Stefan's main role is as Accounts Receivable Clerk, he is keen to get involved with, and will gladly take on, additional tasks due to him currently studying for his AAT exams. Currently, he performs the following tasks:

- Opens the post alone (which may include cheques received from customers)
- Monitors the email account for notification of customers paying by bank transfer
- Collates and banks the cheques received during his lunch hour
- Raises the sales invoices
- Chases payments from customers

Required

Note any issues with Stefan covering these roles.

Real life example

Think about a large retail organisation such as Marks & Spencer or Boots. They have many branches and lots of information on sales, inventory, deliveries and customer orders to collate. Both these companies have central finance functions which allow them to focus on specific areas. For example, Boots has a treasury function which is solely in charge of verifying cash flow, investing excess funds, identifying areas for further funding and advising senior management regarding large investments and their timing. If the treasury function also tried to maintain the sales orders, given the scale of the organisation, this would soon become very muddled.

2.4 Levels of management

A key aspect of organisational structure is how many levels of management there are between the leader of the organisation – the chief executive officer (CEO) or managing director (MD) – and the people doing the work.

The structure can be described as either tall or flat.

A **tall** structure has the following characteristics:

- Many levels of management
- Each manager is only responsible for a small number of staff (a narrow span of control)
- Is hierarchical

A **flat** structure has the following characteristics:

- Few levels of management from the bottom of the organisation to the top
- Each manager may have many staff working for them (this is known as a wide span of control)

| Tall organisation | Flat organisation |

The trend in modern organisation structures is to flatten or de-layer organisational structures, removing whole levels of management.

No single structure is right or wrong; it must fit the organisation type and size, and there are advantages and disadvantages of each.

The number of levels from the top of an organisation to the bottom can also be described as the **scalar chain.** A tall organisation will have a longer scalar chain than a flat organisation.

Activity 2: Tall and flat organisation structures

Per the scenario, CCC has a relatively flat structure comprising of the following:

Required

(a) What are the advantages of the flat organisation structure for CCC?

(b) Consider the impact on the company if CCC added another two layers of management to make the organisation 'taller'. What benefits or issues could arise?

Real life example: NHS

The NHS is a very large organisation which has many layers of management, so is a good example of a 'tall' structure. It has a wide range of stakeholders, including employees (who range from experienced doctors and surgeons through to porters and cleaners) and external stakeholders (patient groups, fundraising bodies, regulatory bodies).

The advantages of the NHS's tall organisation structure include the following:

*   Narrow span of control – making it easier for management to manage their subordinates
*   Clear management structure
*   Clear lines of responsibilities
*   Clear lines of control – essential for patient safety
*   Employees can see a clear career progression ladder, which can feel more achievable
*   This type of structure is suited to larger organisations

2.5 Culture of the accounting function

The accounting function is not just the accounting system plus the employees who operate it. A key element of any accounting function is the culture that exists within it.

KEY TERM

> **Culture:** This is 'the way we do things around here'. It may be very different from the way a company might ideally want it to be.

Managers and owners set the standard for the accounting function because they operate it on a day to day basis, and therefore determine its culture. This is often what makes one company and its accounting function different from another.

The culture of the accounting function may be:

(a)   Based on **teamwork** – where everyone helps each other to ensure all tasks are completed on time and appropriately by the team as a whole

(b)   Based on **individualism** – where each member of staff sticks to their own roles and responsibilities

(c)   Based on **control** – where all rules and procedures are adhered to at all times. The control environment at an organisation will impact on how many and how often the levels of management interact with the staff

(d)   **Laissez-faire** (relaxed) – where controls are informal and trust is an important part of the control framework

No particular culture is right or wrong, but a certain culture may be inappropriate to the accounting function in question eg a laissez-faire culture in respect of cash is always risky.

The culture of an organisation may change with personnel or technological changes, such as a new managing director or head of department, or a new integrated software system being installed.

Activity 3: Culture

Consider the two examples stated above (CCC and the NHS).

Required

What key differences would you expect to find between the cultures of the accounting functions within these two organisations?

2.6 Ethics and sustainability

You will have been introduced to the ethical aspects of working in the Level 3 *Business Awareness* unit. The ethical outlook of a profit-seeking company will play a role in formulating the culture of an organisation, eg a commitment to minimising carbon emissions will influence its manufacturing and procurement policies. In relation to their work in an accounting function, remember that an accountant must consider:

(a) **Economic aspects:**

    (i) Supporting their company to be profitable

    (ii) Looking for ways to improve the efficiency of the accounting function and the company generally

(b) **Social aspects:**

    (i) Supporting policies on corporate governance

    (ii) Supporting local businesses when choosing suppliers and paying them on time

    (iii) Consulting the local community when making decisions, eg investing in existing premises or relocating operations

(c) **Environmental aspects:**

    (i) Supporting their company to use less energy, reduce pollution and manage resources and relationships with a view of the long term

    (ii) Running the accounting function in a sustainable manner, eg not printing emails unless necessary, turning lights off at the end of the day and recycling materials where possible

3 Staffing structures within the accounting function

Accounting functions within companies can be centralised or decentralised. Some organisations may have limited staff or experience and so look to outsource some activities, such as payroll or debt collection.

3.1 Centralisation of the accounting function

> **Centralised accounting function:** All accounting tasks are performed at head office, regardless of where the company's other activities are carried out.

All the data is stored at a central location and accounting function staff process it centrally, although this may be by accessing the system from many different locations. All departments in the company are served by this one accounting function.

Staff will be trained according to the department and role they work in, and will have acquired highly specialised knowledge, resulting in increased efficiency.

3.2 Decentralised accounting function

Decentralised accounting function: Data is stored and processed locally, and perhaps independently by staff at different locations or with different computer networks.

In decentralised accounting functions, there is no link between processes, each being formed independently of the others.

Staff will need to have a broader awareness of what roles they may be working on; sometimes training and actual job roles will vary between sites, eg the Manchester office may have different working practices and even a different culture to the Southend office within the same organisation.

Activity 4: Centralised accounting function

CCC is proposing to open new stores along the South coast of England. Rather than having several administration offices, they are looking to use their current accounting team to manage their expanded operations.

Required

List the advantages and disadvantages of CCC having a centralised accounting function. Conclude and recommend whether CCC should operate a centralised or decentralised accounting function based upon the information you have been given.

3.3 Outsourcing the accounting function

Many organisations centralise some, or more rarely all, of the tasks carried out by an accounting function and then outsource this work to a third party, often under strict contractual agreements known as service level agreements (SLAs).

Outsourcing: Where an organisation arranges for essential, but often routine or specialised, tasks to be carried out by a third party.

Outsourcing of accounting functions is most popular for routine tasks, such as payroll, which:

- Are highly automated
- Rely on information technology for processing
- Require highly specialised and up-to-date skills, knowledge or technology

An example is the 'buying in' of the specialised knowledge from a payroll bureau, common in many smaller entities. This shares the cost of specialised software and skilled staff across several companies, producing economies of scale and a cheaper service for all customers. Other areas which may be outsourced include legal services, human resource and debt collection.

Activity 5: Outsourcing

Sonja Douglas (Wages Clerk)

Sonja joined CCC eight months ago. Although Sonja is willing to work some extra hours if required, she does not want to commit herself to any more permanent hours. Sonja gained a qualification in payroll four years ago, but has never progressed any further or taken any other development courses. She currently works two full days a week.

Stefan Kalinowski (Accounts Receivable Clerk)

Stefan was employed one year ago. He works four days a week, and has chosen not to work Fridays. He has been studying for his AAT exams and is currently studying Level 3. He has an excellent academic background, with one of his A Levels being in accountancy. This is his first accountancy-related role.

Margaret Peterson (Senior Accounts Clerk)

Margaret joined the company 18 months ago (application letter on file but no CV). She is employed on a part-time basis of five half days per week. She has 15 years' experience of working in an accounts office, but no formal qualifications. She has limited experience of working with accounting software.

Required

Write brief notes highlighting where CCC could benefit from outsourcing some of its accounting functions.

4 Stakeholders of organisations

To understand why financial reports are produced, it is important to first consider who the users of the accounts will be. Some reports are used for external reporting purposes, eg statement of profit or loss, and others for internal use only eg budgetary reports.

4.1 Types of stakeholder

> **Stakeholder:** Individuals or groups that, potentially, have an interest in what the company does.

A stakeholder is anyone who is affected by the actions of the organisation.

Stakeholders can be:

- Internal or external to the organisation eg banks (external) and shareholders (internal)
- Directly or indirectly affected by its actions (eg customers, suppliers, employees, beneficiaries)

4.2 Information requirements of stakeholders

Each type of stakeholder has a different role in relation to the organisation and, therefore, has different informational needs.

Organisations need to communicate appropriately with stakeholders. The accounting function and accounting systems of the organisation are often the key source of the information they require.

A stakeholder that has a high level of interest in the organisation and also a high level of power – for instance, a bank that has given the organisation a large overdraft and is concerned that it is about to be breached – should be regarded as a key player when it comes to giving it the information it seeks. Organisations in this position should make sure that they keep the bank well informed, and perhaps even involved in its decisions (eg authorising large items of capital expenditure).

Other stakeholders, with lower levels of interest and/or power, should simply be kept informed to the degree required by legislation or contractual requirements, eg small shareholders should be sent copies of the annual financial statements and invited to the annual general meeting (AGM) as required by company law.

4.3 Internal stakeholders

> **Internal stakeholders:** This category of stakeholders includes employees, management and owners (eg shareholders).

They will require different types of information, depending on their role within the organisation, for example management and owners will want to know how the organisation is performing but will not necessarily need to have a detailed view of what payments any given customer has made on their account. Equally, a payables ledger clerk will need to know which invoices are required to be paid on the next payment run, and so will need a detailed schedule for review on a supplier - by-supplier basis.

Information provided to internal stakeholders is not formalised by regulatory or legal guidance; instead, the users will dictate what information they require and how they want this to be presented to ensure the most efficient way of using it for their own needs.

Internal stakeholders may be using the system to ensure that they can perform their jobs correctly. For example, warehouse staff will need to be able to access the inventory system to check availability or location of stock, sales staff will need to be able to access price and available stock information, as well as accounts receivable to ensure that any credit extended to customers is appropriate.

Staff hours are increasingly being logged using computer systems, such as a card swipe system in factories and online timesheets for office-based staff. This is useful information for management as they pay staff for the hours they have worked, but they can also ensure accurate costing of finished goods (labour rates and efficiencies) and job costings (such as solicitors' and accountants' charge out rates).

Activity 6: Internal stakeholders

Consider the following list of internal stakeholders. Note down the information which they would specifically require as employees of CCC.

(1)   Directors of CCC

(2)   Joe Bloggins in his role as warehouse manager

(3)   Joe Bloggins in his role as operations manager

(4)   Wages clerk

Required

Explain how each of the stakeholders above would use the information they require and, where appropriate, consider any risks to the business if the information they receive is inaccurate or late.

4.4 External stakeholders

> **External stakeholders:** This group of stakeholders includes customers, suppliers, banks and public groups.

They will usually require a more formal and standardised reporting format. If the organisation has a bank loan or overdraft, the bank will want to review the financial statements as well as any business forecasts.

Statutory financial reports must be filed with the Registrar of Companies on an annual basis in line with the Companies Act 2006 and appropriate accounting standards and policies.

Activity 7: External stakeholders

Using the pre-seen information provided on CCC, identify the key external stakeholders who would require information regularly from the company. Briefly explain why these stakeholders would require this information.

5 External reporting requirements

Financial reports are used by internal and external stakeholders. External reports will generally have to adhere to a set of reporting requirements laid down in company law and presented in accordance with the applicable financial reporting framework. Internal reports can be less formalised and will be set out according to the type and the needs of the individual organisation.

You will have covered the content, legal and regulatory requirements of external reports in Level 4 *Drafting and Interpreting Financial Statements*.

5.1 Statutory financial statements

International Financial Reporting Standards ('IFRS® Standards') are updated regularly. As such, it is important that any organisation which uses them to compile their financial statements can accurately compile the financial information.

The purpose and importance of statutory financial statements prepared in accordance with the Companies Act 2006 and accounting standards has been covered in *Drafting and Interpreting Financial Statements*. Here is a brief recap of the key purposes:

(a) To determine whether the organisation has made a profit or a loss

(b) To demonstrate how well (or otherwise) the directors have exercised their management or ' stewardship' of the company's resources

(c) To meet the company's statutory requirement to prepare financial statements that show a true and fair view of its financial performance during a period, and its financial position at the end of it

(d) To help shareholders (and potential new investors) evaluate how far their capital invested in the company is at risk, and determine the return they should be expecting to compensate them for this risk

(e) To help lenders and suppliers determine whether the company will be able to meet its financial commitments as they fall due

The statutory financial statements comprise the following:

KEY TERM

Statement of financial position: A list of all of the assets, liabilities and equity of the business at a particular point in time (the end of the reporting period).

Statement of profit or loss: A summary of the activity of the company during the reporting period (usually a year).

Statement of changes in equity: A reconciliation of the opening and closing equity balances for the reporting period. It enables stakeholders to see the impact of new share issues, profit or loss for the period and dividends paid to equity shareholders.

Statement of cash flows: An analysis of how and why the company's cash balance has changed during a reporting period. In addition to the statement of financial position and the statement of profit or loss, it is important for both management and current and potential investors to understand how cash is being utilised by the business.

Activity 8: Financial statements

CCC has a December year end. The pre-seen information has extracts from the previous year's financial statements.

Required

Identify the reports which would be most useful to the external stakeholders identified in Activity 7.

Highlight any potential issues that may arise in respect of these stakeholders using the financial statements and whether any further information will be required by them in addition to the financial statements.

Activity 9: Cash flows

The following is an extract from the statement of cash flows produced by CCC as at 31 December 20X2. It was produced as part of the pack supplied by the external accountants, Bright & Co. The Cookridge brothers are very pleased to have a statement of cash flows; however, they are unsure how to interpret it.

CCC Ltd

Statement of cash flows for the year ended 31 December 20X2

	£	£
Cash flows from operating activities		
Profit before tax		2,000
Add back		
Depreciation for 20X2	7,000	
Finance costs	5,000	
Increase in inventory	(24,000)	
Increase in receivables	(51,000)	
Increase in payables	47,000	
		(16,000)
Cash used in operating activities		(14,000)
Less		
Interest paid		(5,000)
Net cash used in operating activities		(19,000)
Cash flows from investing activities		

	£	£
Purchase of non-current assets	(2,000)	
Net cash used in investing activities		(2,000)
Cash flows from financing activities		
Receipt of loan	60,000	
Net cash generated from financing activities		60,000
Net increase in cash and cash equivalents		39,000
Cash and cash equivalents @ 1 January 20X2		(74,000)
Cash and cash equivalents @ 31 December 20X2		(35,000)

Required

Briefly explain the significance of the key figures in the CCC statement of as at 31 December 20X2. Use specific examples from the statement to support your answer.

5.2 Tax regulations

Financial statements are not the only external reporting requirement; the local tax authorities will need to ensure that the organisation is paying sufficient tax based on their profits for the period.

The main taxes for organisations are corporation tax and VAT (Value Added Tax). For *Internal Accounting Systems and Controls*, you will not be asked detailed computational questions, but you will need to understand the reporting implications on the organisation.

HMRC require most employers to report their payroll deductions on a monthly basis, using Real Time Information ('RTI'). This requires organisations to use software that can report this information to HMRC online. It also requires organisations to report on a timely basis, placing both technological and staff burdens on businesses, as information is required prior to payments to staff being made.

Since 2019, VAT must also be reported electronically for all VAT-registered businesses, again requiring upgraded software (or even new software in some cases) and additional training time for staff.

5.3 Other government legislation

Pensions legislation has been introduced whereby employers are required to auto-enrol their staff into stakeholder pension schemes. This has resulted in additional financial burdens (payment of contributions) and administrative burdens (ensuring all staff are enrolled within the reporting deadlines and submitting the required returns to the Pensions Regulator) on the payroll staff within the finance function.

Money Laundering Regulations were updated in 2017, requiring organisations to register with a supervisory authority (such as the AAT) and ensuring compliance with the strict reporting criteria, as well as organisations to ensure additional training of staff to identify and prevent the main elements of money laundering or terrorist financing. In particular, the Regulation requires an organisation to have documented policies, controls and procedures in place to prevent activities related to money laundering.

6 Internal reporting requirements

6.1 Management accounting

Management accounts are not bound by regulation and are intended to meet the needs primarily of the company's management.

The types of management accounting reports are covered in depth in Level 4 *Applied Management Accounting*.

These include the preparation of information such as:

- Budgets
- Standard costs
- Variance analysis
- Ratio analysis
- Sales figures for products and/or divisions
- Inventory levels
- Profitability reports
- Any other internal information prepared using financial data

Management accounting reports will be used internally by decision makers to help them:

(a) Make decisions on resourcing and resource allocation

(b) Manage the company's profitability and cash flow, for example, strong accounts receivable and credit control systems will ensure that prompt payment ('settlement') discounts are taken up when available, and creditors are paid on time

(c) Monitor the controls and review any areas for unusual or unexpected results which may highlight business-critical issues, control issues or potential fraud. This is covered in more detail in Chapter 5

Organisations should be taking advantage of available tax incentives, too. For example, when considering a new large non-current asset to be purchased, what are the capital allowances available, and does this affect the decision to proceed with the purchase?

Management must carefully monitor the spending of government grants to ensure adequate reporting in the financial statements as well as accurate comparison of actuals against budget.

6.2 Budgetary control reports

A key report issued by the management accounting function is the **budgetary control report**, or variance analysis report.

A budgetary control report compares standard costs and revenues with actual results to obtain variances which highlight any deviations that managers should investigate to improve performance.

Activity 10: CCC budget control report

Below is the budgetary control report for the newly launched Wood Effect (Oak) in the Umteeko range for quarter 1 of 20X3. CCC only prepares this once a quarter due to the level of work required and the ability of the staff to complete this in addition to their current workloads. Stefan, who has some AAT training, is responsible for completing this analysis. Stefan does not fully understand how fixed costs are absorbed, so he has left those bits blank for now. Stefan has included the cost of delivery and motor expenses in the variable cost calculation.

This analysis covers only the best-selling products and is passed to the directors for their review. However, Stefan is unsure as to which areas are of most interest to the directors.

CCC Ltd

Budgetary control report for Umteeko Oak the three months to March 20X3

	£	£	£	
Budgeted profit			21,000	
Sales volume profit variance			1,750	(Favourable)
Standard profit from actual sales			22,750	
	Favourable	Adverse		
Variances				
Sales price	975			
Material price	200			
Material usage		7,500		
Labour rate	600			
Labour efficiency		4,250		
Variable overhead rate	125			
Variable overhead efficiency	350			
Fixed overhead expenditure	–			
Fixed overhead volume efficiency	–			
Fixed overhead volume capacity	–			
	2,250	11,750	9,500	(Adverse)
Actual profit			13,250	

Required

(a) Identify areas on which the directors should focus in more detail in the above budgetary control report.

(b) Comment on any limitations on the above budgetary information supplied.

The mechanics of how the standard costs are determined, and how the associated variances are calculated, are covered in the Level 4 *Applied Management Accounting* unit, so are not covered here. The management accounting unit also covers the meaning of these variances, and how they complement each other.

Understanding and communicating these aspects of the budgetary report are vital roles of the accounting function.

7 Ethical and sustainability reporting

Aside from profitability and cash flow, organisations are increasingly being assessed by internal and external stakeholders on their ethical and sustainable practices and policies.

There are various ways in which the organisation can report performance and more generally communicate with its stakeholders on these matters.

7.1 Mission statement

> **Mission statement:** A statement of a company's main objective, and its purpose, strategy and values.

Mission statements are published for the benefit of employees and other stakeholders of the organisation. There is no standard format, but mission statements should generally be:

- **Brief** – to help ensure they are easy to understand and remember
- **Flexible** – to help accommodate change
- **Distinctive** – to make the organisation stand out

7.2 Corporate social reporting (CSR)

Increasingly, organisations are being assessed on how they are acting as 'good corporate citizens'.

> **Corporate social responsibility reports:** Outline the objectives for ensuring the ethical, sustainable and moral aims and achievements of the organisation.

These corporate social reports (CSR) are usually included within the annual report, and discuss their policies in terms of ethical, environmental, charitable and sustainability factors. Larger companies must report on their social and environmental activities and sustainability impact via dedicated CSR statements embedded within their financial statements. However, smaller companies are also publicising their policies to differentiate themselves from competitors. Although the detailed content is outside of the syllabus, you will need to have an understanding of how ethical and sustainability information has an impact on stakeholders.

Real life example: Jaguar Land Rover

Jaguar Land Rover takes its corporate social responsibility reporting very seriously and aims to provide as much information as possible regarding its aims, its results to date and where it sees that it can develop in the future.

- The annual report contains a statement of environmental and social responsibility.
- New Reimagine Strategy:
    - Becoming an all-electric luxury brand from 2025
    - Achieving a net zero carbon emissions across the supply chain, products and operations by 2039
- Environmental reporting (waste, water usage, recycling, emissions)
- Community projects (staff volunteering to assist with local projects)
- 'Building British' and how it supports the local economies
- Sourcing ethically sourced/recycled materials for the manufacturing of new cars (it uses recycled aluminium)

By putting this information in the public domain, Jaguar is aiming to be transparent about how it performs in ethical, environmental and sustainability terms as well as financially as a company.

(Jaguar Land Rover, 2020)

7.3 Sustainability reporting

There are six main responsibilities of the accounting function in regard to upholding the principles of sustainability:

(a) Creating and promoting an ethical culture within the company
   - Supporting ethical policies as they are introduced
   - Discouraging and reporting illegal or unethical practices (money laundering, fraud, theft, bribery, non-compliance with regulations, bullying and short-term decision making)
(b) Championing the aims of sustainability within the context of the company's culture and its own policies on sustainability
(c) Evaluating and quantifying reputational and other ethical risks
(d) Taking social, environmental and ethical factors into account when preparing information for decision-making and performance measurement
(e) Promoting sustainable practices in relation to products and services, customers, employees, the workplace, the supply chain, and business functions and processes
(f) Raising awareness of social responsibility

7.4 Ethical reporting

Organisations may also have ethical values, based on the norms and standards of behaviour that their leaders believe will best help them express their identity and achieve their objectives. Often the ethical values of the company are set out in its mission statement.

Setting standards is important as organisations are responsible for their actions and can be held accountable for the effects of their actions on people and society. Often these standards are not legally binding, rather they are guidelines for specific industries to ensure best practice.

As such individual organisations should behave ethically towards any employees, customers, suppliers and communities affected by the decisions and actions that they take.

The Groceries Supply Code of Practice (GSCoP) is not a legal requirement for supermarkets, however, it outlines and makes recommendations upon retailers regarding fair payment times, supply agreements and rules regarding deductions (including marketing, penalties and delays).

Supermarkets which perform poorly are likely to be questioned by shareholders at AGMs, receive bad publicity and potentially lose sales or contracts with suppliers.

Increasingly, large companies are disclosing their ethical treatment of suppliers in their Annual Reports.

 Real life example

> **Groceries (Supply Chain Practices) Market Investigation Order 2009 (the Order) and the Groceries Supply Code of Practice (GSCOP)**
>
> Waitrose is subject to the Groceries (Supply Chain Practices) Market Investigation Order 2009 (the "Order") and the Groceries Supply Code of Practice ("GSCOP" also referred to as the "Code").
>
> Both the Order and, in particular, the Code, regulates Waitrose's everyday trading relationships with our grocery suppliers, ensuring that as a Designated Retailer, we treat our suppliers fairly and in accordance with the Code. The Order also includes provisions on training requirements for our buyers, mandates a need for agreements to be in place with all our groceries suppliers and that any such agreements incorporate the Code. These principles, and the desire to treat our suppliers fairly, are also enshrined within our Principle 6 and Rule 96 of the John Lewis Partnership's Constitution and are therefore in keeping with the Partnership's general ethos.
>
> As required by the Order, the Waitrose Code Compliance Officer ("CCO") is obliged to present a report detailing our compliance to the Code to the Partnership's Audit and Risk Committee, for onwards submission to the Competition and Markets Authority ("CMA"). The reporting period covered was 26 January 2020 to 30 January 2021 and was submitted to the CMA on 13 April 2021.
>
> (Source: John Lewis Partnership Annual Report 2021)

In the extract above from the John Lewis Partnership Annual Report, Waitrose confirms that it adheres to the GSCoP, and also highlighted that there had been an increase in queries by suppliers. The organisation also states that they have a specific committee to monitor the treatment of suppliers, and so placing emphasis on its importance to John Lewis and Waitrose.

7.5 Integrated reporting

It is clear that many businesses need to report more than just figures and financial results in their annual reports. With over 70% of consumers stating that they will prefer to use the service of more ethical companies, and over a third stating that would be happy to pay more to ensure that the companies they use are ethical ('Accounting for Good', AAT, 2016), it is clear that reporting in a more 'holistic' manner is increasingly important for modern businesses.

Integrated reporting <IR> is a way of reporting financial, ethical and sustainable factors, usually including information on the welfare of staff, assistance to the local community and the business's impact on the environment.

You will not be expected to produce an integrated report in your assessment, but you should be aware that this is one of the ways that businesses can report performances, both with financial and non-financial parameters in their annual report.

Activity 11: Ethical and sustainability information

The following are some extracts from the directors' report contained in CCC's financial statements for the year ended 31 December 20X2, together with the company's mission statement.

CCC mission statement

Our mission is to provide an excellent level of service to all of our customers – and we endeavour to offer our customers a quality product at a competitive price.

We aim to act ethically towards our suppliers, customers and staff, ensuring the best in service and supporting diverse needs and requirements.

The environment is important to us and we aim to recycle wherever possible; we promise to remove all of the packaging from customers' premises, and dispose of this in an environmentally friendly way."

Extract from the directors' report as at 31 December 20X2

Revenue has increased year on year, but margins on the sale and fitting of carpets have been affected by challenging market conditions with larger national firms' aggressive price promises affecting what we can demand for our products and services.

We have recently introduced a vinyl reclamation scheme which can recycle the offcuts from vinyl rolls. The company recycles the off cuts into making traffic cones. A small charge is made for this however, this has reduced our non-recyclable waste costs.

Due to a new contract with Umteeko, we are looking to expand our stores across the south coast of England as this is proving to be a very popular product.

Required

Identify the following:

(1) Ethical information provided by the directors and the mission statement

(2) Sustainability information provided by the directors and the mission statement

(3) The stakeholders who are most likely to be interested in this information

Ethical information	Sustainability information	Stakeholder

8 Management information systems (MIS)

Management Information: Information provided to management to help them with planning, controlling, performance measurement and decision making.

Management Information System (MIS): The processing of the various information using computers and computer software from multiple departments or functions.

Most of the information produced by the accounting function for both internal and external stakeholders is based on data about the transactions that it has processed over a given period. These are recorded in the accounting system, which we will look at in the next chapter.

However, some of the data comes from the wider **management information system (MIS)**. This is particularly the case when the accounting function is preparing information for its key internal stakeholder, the management of the company.

8.1 Purposes of management information

All companies require management information for a range of purposes including:

- Planning
- Control
- Performance measurement
- Decision making

To plan effectively managers, need information that helps them make decisions about what should and can be done bearing in mind:

- The resources that are available
- Timescales and deadlines imposed
- The likely outcomes under alternative scenarios

To control performance, management need information to assess whether operations are proceeding as planned or whether there is some unexpected deviation from the plan. If so, they may need to take some form of corrective action.

Just as individual operations need to be controlled, so overall performance must be measured and reported, in a budgetary control report or a scorecard.

Good-quality information should lead to better-informed decisions across the range.

The larger the organisation, the more robust the systems required. Lots of information will need to be processed and then organised in a way which makes it usable by management.

8.2 Types of information

Different types and quantities of information are required by managers for different purposes.

Operational information: Used to ensure that specific tasks are planned and carried out properly within a factory or office. The operational level would deal with cash receipts and payments, bank reconciliations and so forth.

Tactical information: Used to decide how the resources of the business should be deployed, and to monitor how efficiently they are being used. The tactical level would deal with cash flow forecasts and working capital management.

Strategic information: Used to (a) plan the objectives of the company and (b) assess whether the objectives are being met in practice.

8.3 Information requirements in different industry sectors

The following are some typical information requirements of a manufacturing company and a service sector company.

8.3.1 Manufacturing company

Information type	Examples
Strategic	Future demand estimates New product development plans Competitor analysis
Tactical	Variance analysis Departmental accounts Inventory turnover
Operational	Production reject rate Materials and labour used Inventory levels

The information requirements of commercial companies are influenced by the need to make and monitor profit.

Information that contributes to the following measures is important:

- Changeover times
- Number of common parts
- Level of product diversity
- Product and process quality

8.3.2 Service sector company

Information type	Examples
Strategic	Forecast sales growth and market share Profitability Capital structure
Tactical	Resource utilisation such as average staff time charged out, number of customers per hairdresser Customer satisfaction rating
Operational	Staff timesheets Customer waiting time Individual customer feedback

Companies are customer and results oriented. As a consequence, the difference between service and other companies' information requirements has decreased. Businesses have realised that most of their activities can be measured, and many can be measured in similar ways regardless of the business sector.

Activity 12: Sector analysis

CCC is a small retail business specialising in carpets and flooring. The management team have a background in this sector.

Consider some of the information that management would need to look at in more detail to help them plan future budgets or amend longer-term plans.

Required

Complete the table below, using information from the pre-seen scenario and considering the sort of information a company would need to have in order to grow and become more successful in their sector.

Information type	Examples
Strategic	
Tactical	
Operational	

8.4 Performance indicators

A key way in which statutory financial statements are analysed by both internal and external stakeholders is the application of **ratio analysis**.

Ratio analysis is making comparisons between figures in a company's financial statements and how they relate to each other in order to determine the financial performance and position of the company.

The mechanics of how ratios are calculated are covered in the Level 4 *Drafting and Interpreting Financial Statements* unit so are not discussed in detail here. However, a list of examinable ratios and how they should be calculated is included for reference purposes:

Ratio	Calculation
Gross profit margin	(Gross profit ÷ Revenue) × 100 = X%
Operating profit margin	(Profit from operations ÷ Revenue) × 100 = X%
Current ratio	(Current assets ÷ Current liabilities) = X :1
Quick (acid test) ratio	([Current assets - Inventories] ÷ Current liabilities) = X :1
Inventory turnover	(Cost of sales ÷ Inventories) = X times
Inventory holding period (days)	(Inventories ÷ Cost of sales) × 365 = X days
Trade receivables collection period (days)	(Receivables ÷ Revenue) × 365 = X days
Trade payables collection period (days)	(Payables ÷ Cost of sales) × 365 = X days
Gearing	(Non-current liabilities ÷ [Total equity + Non-current liabilities]) × 100 = X%
Return on capital employed (ROCE)	(Profit from operations ÷ [Total equity + Non-current liabilities]) × 100 = X%

8.5 Changes to management information

The management information required in an organisation is likely to change over time.

Management information systems should be reviewed regularly to ensure that the information provided to management is relevant to the current organisation. As an organisation grows, or the product mix changes, different management information will be required to make the best-informed decisions.

Chapter summary

- The accounting function aims to process transactions so it can provide information to meet stakeholder needs.
- The accounting system and information required by an organisation will depend on its size. A small charity will have different requirements to a multinational retail business.
- Sections of a large accounting function are: transaction processing; financial accounting; management accounting and treasury management.
- Management structures will vary according to the business need and the culture of the organisation. A tall structure will have many layers of management, whilst a flat structure will have fewer levels of management.
- A major aspect of the accounting function is whether it is centralised, so the same function serves all parts of the company, or decentralised, so different departments etc have their own accounting functions.
- Centralised accounting functions enable the accounting to be completed at one site. This can ensure efficiency in terms of producing information and liaising with other departments. However, it can also mean that the accountants are 'far removed' from the rest of the business.
- Often businesses will outsource repetitive activities or activities requiring a high level of specialism. A smaller organisation is likely to outsource more technical work, such as tax or legal assistance. A larger organisation may outsource more mundane or repetitive tasks such as batch invoice processing.
- An organisation has a range of stakeholders: internal (managers, employees and shareholders) and external (bankers, suppliers, customers, government and local community).
- Stakeholders have differing information needs, and it is the role of the accounting function to provide that information.
- The company's statutory financial statements serve a number of purposes: to identify profit or loss; to demonstrate the directors' stewardship; to comply with statute; to help shareholders evaluate their investment; to help bankers/suppliers determine the company's ability to pay on time; to help government/regulators determine the company's compliance with its regulatory obligations; and to provide information about the company more widely.
- Statutory financial statements comprise statements of a statement of profit or loss, a statement of financial position, a statement of changes in equity and a statement of cash flows.
- Financial statements are not the only external reporting requirement, HMRC will need to ensure that the organisation is paying sufficient tax based on their profits for the period.
- Management accounts provide information to internal stakeholders so that they can make decisions on resourcing, and manage the company's profitability and cash flow.
- Management information systems (MIS) are designed according to the need of the organisation. These will vary in complexity but essentially all MIS must allow the organisation to effectively plan, control, measure performance and enable decision making.
- The types of management information which are required are strategic, operational and tactical and vary according to industry.

Activity answers

Activity 1: Multitasking in a small organisation

CCC is a small company with a small department of mainly part-time staff and so it is difficult for it in its current process to ensure adequate controls and ensure supervision.

Stefan is in charge of the whole receivables process, from the raising of invoices through to the collection and banking of cheques. It would not be difficult for an individual in this capacity to 'skim' some of the receivable monies and write off any balance on the customer accounts.

Equally, as he opens the post alone, there is a risk that cheques may go missing or be miscounted when they arrive in the post room.

A small organisation may lack the resources to effect complete segregation of duties, but a director or another accounts clerk could act as a second signatory to confirm the cheques have arrived or bank the cheques instead of Stefan.

Activity 2: Tall and flat organisation structures

(a) Advantages of the flat organisation structure for CCC:

- More freedom and responsibility for employees
- Quicker decision making by CCC that is not hindered by referring up many levels of management
- Quicker communication from top to bottom
- Reduced cost of management
- Less bureaucracy

(b) Adding additional layers to the management structure at CCC could result in the following:

- More time for the directors to focus on the strategic and long-term plans for CCC, rather than getting involved in the detailed day-to-day business of the company.
- Possible resentment from members of staff who like the flatter structure and do not want additional bureaucracy or increased controls in their working processes.
- A new level of management could provide additional controls, experience and management of the staff, especially where staff are mainly part time.
- Many of the advantages outlined above would be lost eg greater management cost in terms of salaries would result.

Activity 3: Culture

CCC

As CCC is a smaller organisation, there is likely to be more of a focus on teamwork as people will be expected to cover other employees' roles. The accounting department is small so, if Sonja, the wages clerk is on holiday, another employee, such as John or Peter Cookridge would have to help out. This is likely to result in a more relaxed atmosphere based on the trust of individuals to report accurately their hours and to help out when needed.

NHS

There are lots of levels of bureaucracy here, likely to have more formalised rules and reporting structure. Rules and procedures are likely to be strongly adhered to, especially as their main role is regarding the health of the public.

Activity 4: Centralised accounting function

Advantages of CCC having a centralised accounting function:

- Greater economies of scale as fewer staff overall are needed to complete the same amount of work

- Economies of scope as all departments benefit from having highly trained, expert accounting staff servicing their requirements.

- Consistency of approach as processes are only performed once

- Standardised consistent procedures

- Decisions can be made taking into account the 'big picture' (eg the impact on the company as a whole).

- Major decisions on expenditure and investment such as recruitment can be centrally controlled.

Disadvantages of CCC having a centralised accounting function:

- Analysis and decision making are remote from operational centres.

- There is little or no direct involvement with the rest of the company.

- It may lack relevant expertise if other departments are developing innovative business methods.

CCC is better suited to a centralised system so that all staff can be trained to use one system and can then cover each other's roles or access information if required. It will also enable financial reports to be quickly generated and easily provided to the joint owners for decision making.

Activity 5: Outsourcing

Payroll preparation/Human Resource management

- The experience of Sonja, the wages clerk, is relatively limited and she has no HR experience.

- Issues may arise if an employee has a complex issue, such as long-term sickness, maternity pay or disciplinary procedures, all of which the current wages clerk would struggle to deal with.

- There is a risk that the payroll methodology and calculation is not up to date as Sonja has not undertaken any further training since she qualified four years ago.

- Using a payroll bureau may be more expensive, but this will correct any errors made by the current staff as well as ensuring a strict segregation of duties in this high risk area. Alternatively, a payroll bureau using up-to-date software and skilled staff may be able to perform these tasks in less time that Sonja takes, so may work out cheaper as well as better for CCC.

Financial statements and taxation preparation

- There are no fully qualified accountants in the team so accurate preparation of the financial statements and the taxation requirements may be beyond the capability of the current staff. Areas such as corporate taxation have complex requirements which means that CCC may be missing out on tax breaks or allowances or filing returns incorrectly.

Legal advice

- There is minimal legal experience in the accounting department. This may become an issue for CCC if supplier or employee contracts need to be amended or legal issues arise, such as customer payment disputes or employee discrimination claims.

Activity 6: Internal stakeholders

Directors of CCC

- Management accounts to review the overall performance of the company.
- Aged receivables and payables reports to ensure that payments are being made on time to suppliers and that monies due from customers is being collected on a timely basis. This is necessary for cash flow management.
- Margin analysis on the products or types of products being sold, to verify whether lines should be continued or replaced. Given that the market for carpet is being squeezed and CCC has the local market in the Umteeko range, consider whether the organisation should focus on that longer term.

If this information is not received, there is a risk that the company will not be able to react quickly enough to changes in the market. Cash flow control is vital in a small organisation; if peaks and troughs in cash flow are not correctly managed, the organisation may have to resort to expensive emergency overdrafts or may be unable to take advantage of any bulk order or early settlement discounts which suppliers may offer.

By reviewing the margins and relative profitability of the different types of products, CCC can react more quickly to the market conditions and ensure that they have enough inventory in their more popular lines. Currently, only two members of the fitting team are Umteeko trained which, given the popularity of the product and CCC's regional monopoly on the distribution, seems on the low side. CCC may be at risk of missing an opportunity to develop this line of business to replace its reduced turnover from more traditional floorings, such as carpets and tiles.

Warehouse manager

- Inventory levels – what items are in stock and what has not moved for a long time (this inventory may need to be provided against or written off)
- Sales forecast – what inventory needs to be purchased to ensure that customers receive their products in a timely manner
- Supplier delivery and purchases schedule to ensure that inventory deliveries are as expected and can be verified to what has been ordered, and that there is sufficient room in the warehouse
- Liaison with the operations team to ensure that the inventory will be available when the fitters are booked in to fit the product

Without strict inventory controls, stock may not be in when the fitters are booked in to deliver and fit the products. This will be a waste of resource (fitter time) and risks upsetting the customer who was expecting their carpet or flooring to be fitted on a set date.

Operations manager

- Sales order information to plan the fitters and delivery routes for the week/month ahead
- Vacation details from payroll (to avoid everyone going on holiday at the same time, especially staff with specific skills or training)
- Liaison with the warehouse team to ensure that the inventory will be available when the fitters are booked in to fit the product, otherwise this may cause problems with customer relations in terms of expectation of delivery

Wages clerk

- Details of new starters/leavers
- Information on pay rises authorised by management
- Overtime information authorised by the operations manager, to ensure that overtime is correctly paid on time
- Sales commission information authorised by the sales manager, to ensure that all commission has been verified by the sales manager and paid in a timely manner
- Vacation and sickness details authorised by department managers, to ensure that vacation pay is correctly allocated, and details of sickness (and any sick pay) are logged and monitored

 BPP

- Contracts for all staff (to ensure pay is set at the correct level)
- Cash flow information to ensure that there is sufficient money to pay the staff. If staff cannot be paid on time, there is a risk of employee discontent and losing skilled members of the workforce.

Activity 7: External stakeholders

Key external stakeholders for CCC are likely to include some or all of the following:

- Customers, to ensure that the company is solvent, eg if they have paid their deposit they have some security in CCC being able to supply their product.
- Suppliers, especially any significant or new suppliers who will be assessing CCC for creditworthiness. It will be helpful for CCC's cash flow to be able to buy supplies on credit.
- The Government, including HM Revenue & Customs (HMRC) for PAYE and corporation tax and the Registrar of Companies to ensure that the financial statements are filed on time.
- Lenders, such as the bank. Because CCC has an overdraft and a loan, the lender will monitor CCC's solvency to ensure it is able to pay off its debts.
- Competitors, can access information about CCC as they can view the statutory financial statements from the Registrar of Companies. Although for a small company like CCC the information may be limited to a statement of financial position, and small companies like CCC would want to minimise the amount of information a competitor would be able to view, provided they adhere to financial reporting regulations.
- Regulatory bodies would also be interested in the performance of the organisation, and if a complaint is made against the company there may be further inquiry by consumer groups such as the Citizens Advice Bureau. Poor workmanship may also result in negative reviews on online sites such as TrustedTrader.com
- Umteeko would also have an interest in the performance of CCC. They will be keen to ensure that only trained fitters and approved adhesives are being used with its product. They would also want to view the company's overall performance, as Umteeko relies upon CCC for the sales of their product in the area. There is always a risk for CCC that poor performance on their part could mean that Umteeko decide to use another company to act as their local distributor.

Activity 8: Financial statements

As CCC is a small company, the external reporting information available publicly may be restricted to the statement of financial position and the notes and accounting policies. Nevertheless, this will be of use to the customers, suppliers and lenders as they will be able to verify the solvency of the company. However, this will only be at a certain point in the financial year (31 December) and will not give an up-to-date picture of the financial health of a company.

The bank may require further details, such as management accounts and cash flow statements, to verify that CCC can continue to pay its debts. This information would normally only be available to internal stakeholders. Additionally, there may be specific loan covenants – such as a stated level of interest cover that must be contractually supplied to the lender.

HM Revenue & Customs will want a detailed set of financial statements (companies must now provide detailed financial statements that are not abridged for tax purposes). Again, this information is only produced once a year and is not a guarantee that the tax will be paid on time or whether the company will default on its payments.

HM Revenue & Customs (HMRC) also requires monthly information on the payroll (Real Time Information reporting), which will ensure that payroll deductions are made correctly each month and the monies paid across in a timely manner.

Activity 9: Cash flows

The statement of cash flows separates out the net cash flows during the reporting period arising from:

- Operating activities (profit before tax for the period plus changes in current assets and liabilities excluding non-cash items). Depreciation and finance costs are added back as these are not cash flows from the business so cash used in operating activities was actually a cash outflow of £14,000.

- Movements in working capital as represented by the increase or decrease in the balances for receivables, payables and inventories. In this period, there was a net outflow of £21,000 represented by:

  - Inventory increasing by £24,000, so CCC is holding more stock

  - Receivables increasing by £51,000 as a result of higher sales on credit in the year

  - Payables increasing by £47,000 as a result of increased purchases to support higher sales and inventory levels

- After the interest paid of £5,000 is deducted (there was no tax paid), the net cash used in operating activities of £19,000.

- Investing activities (buying or disposing of non-current assets) so £2,000 was spent on new assets for use in the business.

- Financing activities (paying dividends, taking out or paying back loans, issuing new shares). £60,000 was received from the new loan taken out during the year.

- All of the above cash flows are then reconciled to the opening and closing cash positions – the balance of the cash at hand less the overdraft. At the start of the year there was a cash asset of £4,000 and a cash overdraft of £78,000, so a net cash position of (£74,000). The operating and investing activities of CCC have both result in net cash outflows during the year. However, the receipt of the £60,000 loan has improved the overall cash position during the year so there is a net increase in cash and cash equivalents of £39,000. At 31 December 20X2 there is a £2,000 cash asset and the overdraft has reduced to £37,000, a net cash position of (£35,000).

- The statement therefore summarises where the business has generated its cash in the year, and what it has spent its cash on in the period.

Activity 10: CCC budget control report

(a) Areas of focus

The sales team appear to be exceeding expectations by selling more Umteeko Oak and at a better price than budgeted (£975 favourable variance). However, Stefan should highlight the adverse variances in respect of material usage (£7,500) and labour efficiency (£4,250).

There may be issues with the budgetary process in calculating how much Umteeko Oak is required – for example, a customer may want a 25 m² room covered but this may require more than 25 m² of flooring depending on the shape of the room. From the analysis, the £7,500 adverse material usage variance indicates that either the fitters are using too much Umteeko Oak during the fitting process, or the budget itself is not allowing for realistic levels of wastage eg offcuts.

The £4,250 adverse labour efficiency variance may be related to this. The pre-seen information has highlighted an issue with the lack of fitting time allocated to the Umteeko product. The budget may need to be revised and the sales price amended upwards to reflect the additional time and procedures in fitting this specialist product.

(b) Limitations

The budgetary control report does not show the absorption of fixed costs, which is vital in terms of pricing, as the price charged must cover both fixed and variable costs if a business is to be profitable. If the fixed costs such as rent are not priced into the budget report, then the directors will not fully understand why they are making losses or very small overall profits.

 BPP

Only a certain number of products are currently being monitored due to the limitations of the system (Excel based) and the limited time, experience and judgement of Stefan.

By only selecting a few products, it does not help the directors to fully understand why CCC is struggling financially.

Activity 11: Ethical and sustainability information

Ethical information	Sustainability information	Stakeholder
Mission statement stating CCC's intention to behave ethically towards its customers	Recycling information in the directors' report in the financial statements and the mission statement highlighting its 'green' credentials which is important to any customers who are seeking more sustainable suppliers. Looking to open new stores across the South coast of England, stating that the future is promising and the company is looking ahead to expand further in the region.	Customers
Mission statement stating CCC's intention to behave ethically towards its suppliers	Information regarding CCC's potential move away from carpets and towards vinyl (implicit in the directors' report) may signal to carpet suppliers to offer bigger discounts to CCC or attract other vinyl suppliers to approach CCC.	Suppliers
Mission statement stating that it supports diverse needs and behaves ethically towards its staff may attract new employees with physical or other disabilities to consider CCC when applying for employment	Information in the directors' report implies that the company is a going concern and expansion may offer additional opportunities to staff keen to develop their skills and experience within CCC.	Employees/potential employees
Some investors may want more information regarding the specific ethical actions of the business – for example, some will invest in companies which recycle or have strong 'green' credentials. The mission statement and directors' report both make statements to this effect at CCC.	Information in the directors' report implies, due to the expansion of stores, the contract with Umteeko and its aims to reduce costs that the company should be likely to continue for the foreseeable future. The information also demonstrates that management are aware of the limitations of the current market conditions and what they are doing to mitigate these risks.	Investors and potential investors

Activity 12: Sector analysis

Information type	Examples
Strategic	Forecast sales growth and market share
	Profitability of the different types of product lines – carpet vs vinyl
	Capital structure and gearing analysis (the company is highly geared with the loan and overdraft)
	New stores to be opened in the region; who are the local competition? Does the local economy suit high-quality flooring sold at a premium price, or should it have a discounted store to sell on discontinued lines/offcuts?
	Consideration of independent and national competitors; there is little point in setting up a store next to a large, heavy-discounting national competitor
Tactical	Resource utilisation such as:
	Sales per sales team member
	Commission on a scale based on the type of product that CCC wants to focus on/launch new products, eg focusing on Umteeko products as they have better profit margins, so it makes tactical sense for the salespeople to focus on the products which have higher profit margins
	Material wastage by product (can the flooring be cut in a more economical manner to minimise waste off cuts?)
	Customer satisfaction rating
Operational	Staff timesheets and monitoring of efficiency and utilisation. Does every fitter manage to fit the same amount of flooring over a certain area, or are others better suited to more complex floorings?
	Customer ordering to delivery time
	Individual customer feedback/customer satisfaction survey
	Minimise the cost of waste by increasing recycling and minimising off cut wastage

Test your learning

1 Which of the following statements about the structure of an accounting function is true? Select ONE option.

	✓
A centralised accounting function has better communication with business units than a decentralised one.	
A decentralised accounting function has more economies of scale compared with a centralised one.	
A centralised accounting function has more economies of scope than a decentralised one.	
A decentralised accounting function is better placed to produce group accounts than a centralised one.	

2 Which of the following is LEAST likely to affect the culture of an organisation? Select ONE option.

	✓
Teamwork	
Managers	
Accounting software	
Control environment	

3 Complete the following statement:

A statement of cash flows shows receipt of a loan as part of [▼] and proceeds from the disposal of non-current assets as part of [▼] .

Picklist
- Financing activities
- Investing activities
- Operating activities

4 It is likely that all management decisions will have a financial or economic impact, but organisations also need to consider whether there are other impacts from the decisions made by management. From the options provided, identify the most likely additional impact on the organisation in each scenario.

	Ethical ✓	Environmental ✓
Improving recycling rates in the factory by 30% year on year		
Changing supplier who can supply the materials 20% cheaper, but with less control over the supply chain		

	Ethical ✓	Environmental ✓
Installing a carbon capture unit on the main factory costing £2 million		
Introducing a more generous pension scheme for employees		

5 Which of the following are advantages of a long scalar chain? Tick TWO options

	✓
Fewer direct reports for managers to manager	
Clear lines of responsibility	
Quicker communication from the top management to the bottom of the organisation	
Reduced costs of management	

6 Complete the following statement:

[▼] is used to decide how the resources of the business should be deployed, and to monitor how they are being and have been utilised.

Picklist

- Operational information
- Strategic information
- Tactical information

2 Internal control systems

Learning outcomes

2.1 **Internal controls**

Learners need to understand:

2.1.1 the purpose of internal controls:

- facilitate operations
- safeguard assets
- prevent and detect fraud
- ensure quality of internal and external reporting
- compliance

2.1.2 the types of internal controls used in different parts of the accounting function:

- segregation of duties
- organisational controls
- authorisation and approval
- physical controls
- supervision
- personnel
- arithmetical and accounting
- management

2.1.3 how different types of internal controls suit different types of organisations:

- size (small, medium, large)
- nature (cash-based, credit based, online).

Learners need to be able to:

2.1.4 assess how a strong system of internal controls can minimise the risk of loss to an organisation

2.1.5 assess how a strong system of internal controls can ensure ethical standards in an organisation.

2.2   Prevent and detect fraud and systemic weaknesses

Learners need to understand:

2.2.1 the common types of fraud within a business:

- misappropriation of funds (monetary, inventory)
- misstatement of financial statements (singularity, over time)

2.2.2 systemic weaknesses and their causes:

- lack of controls
- poor implementation controls
- lack of monitoring
- lack of leadership

2.2.3 implications for an organisation if fraud occurs:

- financial
- non-financial

2.2.4 the role of internal controls in:

- preventing fraud and errors
- detecting fraud and errors.

Learners need to be able to:

2.2.5 identify the circumstances when fraud may occur

2.2.6 evaluate the impact of fraud on an organisation:

- financial
- non-financial

2.2.7 assess how internal controls can be used in preventing and detecting fraud

2.2.8 make suggestions for internal controls to prevent and detect fraud

2.2.9 assess the cause of systemic weaknesses in internal control systems.

Assessment context

The topics covered in this chapter will be included within a number of tasks in the Internal Accounting Systems and Controls unit assessment.

Qualification context

The operation of the bookkeeping controls discussed in this chapter is covered at both Level 2 and Level 3.

Business context

The system of internal controls is designed to ensure the company does not fall prey to fraud, error or misstatement of its financial statements. This ensures that the company can operate effectively. The different types of controls within an organisation are identified and explanations as to why they would be important for an accounting system. These are then reviewed in terms of the sales, purchases (including non-current assets) and payroll systems, with activity practice using the CCC scenario.

Chapter overview

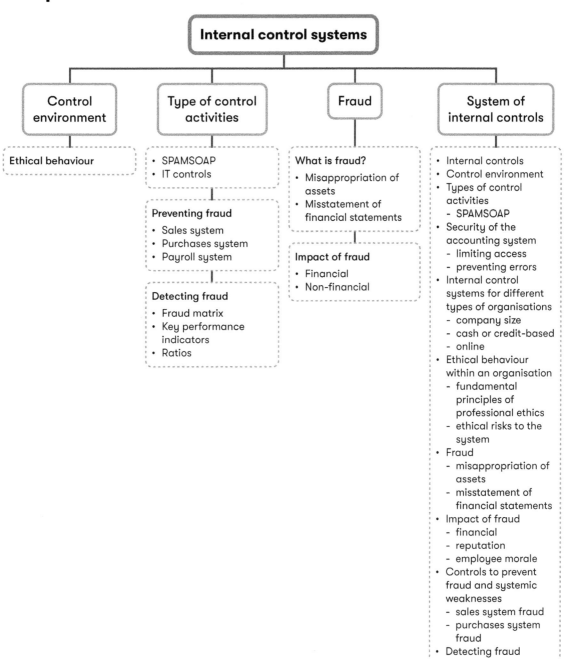

```
                    ┌─────────────────────────────┐
                    │   Internal control systems  │
                    └─────────────────────────────┘
```

Control environment

Ethical behaviour

Type of control activities

- SPAMSOAP
- IT controls

Preventing fraud
- Sales system
- Purchases system
- Payroll system

Detecting fraud
- Fraud matrix
- Key performance indicators
- Ratios

Fraud

What is fraud?
- Misappropriation of assets
- Misstatement of financial statements

Impact of fraud
- Financial
- Non-financial

System of internal controls

- Internal controls
- Control environment
- Types of control activities
  - SPAMSOAP
- Security of the accounting system
  - limiting access
  - preventing errors
- Internal control systems for different types of organisations
  - company size
  - cash or credit-based
  - online
- Ethical behaviour within an organisation
  - fundamental principles of professional ethics
  - ethical risks to the system
- Fraud
  - misappropriation of assets
  - misstatement of financial statements
- Impact of fraud
  - financial
  - reputation
  - employee morale
- Controls to prevent fraud and systemic weaknesses
  - sales system fraud
  - purchases system fraud
- Detecting fraud

Introduction

In this chapter we look at the purpose and type of internal controls commonly found in an organisation.

A strong system of internal controls minimises financial loss within an organisation and can ensure that ethical standards are maintained.

Weak controls are one of the reasons that fraud may occur within an organisation. We will look at the common types of fraud and the implications of fraud within an organisation.

Organisations need to have good internal controls to prevent **fraud** taking place, with particular focus on the importance of the segregation of duties within the accounting function.

Accounting systems are at risk of specific frauds, namely payroll fraud, payables ledger fraud and receivables ledger fraud. We will look at the controls that should be in place to prevent these.

1 Internal controls

> **Internal controls:** Policies and procedures that address the risk that the aims and objectives of the company will not be met.

The purpose of internal controls is to:

- facilitate operations
- safeguard assets
- prevent and detect fraud
- ensure quality of internal and external reporting
- compliance

Internal controls work alongside the control environment to create the overall control framework. This is known as the **system of internal control**.

> **System of internal control:** The control environment, the entity's risk assessment process, the entity's processes to monitor the system of internal control, the information system and communication and control activities.
>
> **Systemic weaknesses:** Weaknesses that arise within the accounting system itself, which leave it open to fraud and error.

Robust systems of internal controls:

- Reduce systemic weaknesses in the accounting system, including the scope for errors
- Reduce the risk of loss or fraud
- Ensure that the accounting system operates appropriately
- Ensure the accounting system can change in line with the environment and organisational requirements
- Ensure that ethical standards are met within an organisation

2 The control environment

> **Control environment:** Formed by the attitudes, awareness and actions of management and those responsible for ensuring that the internal controls within the company meet that company's needs.

The control environment is part of the system of internal controls, alongside the internal controls themselves.

The owners or management of a company must ensure that these control activities are **regularly monitored** to ensure that nothing goes wrong. If the controls are not followed and management do nothing in response, the system of internal controls will not operate effectively, eg if a manager knowingly authorises a fraudulent expense claim by a subordinate, then the internal control requiring expenses to be authorised by management is undermined by the weak control environment.

Management must regularly assess the **existing** system and **identify any new risks** which may affect how robust the control system currently is. Without this monitoring, there is unlikely to be a strong control environment.

Indications of a good control environment include the following:

(a) Management communicate and enforce integrity and ethical behaviour.

(b) Management and staff are well trained and competent.

(c) Management operates in a way that promotes control, eg regularly monitoring whether the controls are working and adhered to in practice.

(d) The company and accounting function is structured in a way that promotes control.

(e) Authority and responsibility for controls is assigned to separate people ie segregation of duties is commonplace.

(f) Human resources policies promote controls.

(g) Management regularly review and reassess any new or potential risks to assess whether the controls in place are robust enough to ensure a strong control environment.

3 Types of control activities

> **Control activities:** Policies and procedures that help ensure that objectives are carried out.
>
> **Segregation of duties:** Making sure that a number of people are involved in different parts of each process to minimise the opportunity for fraud and error.
>
> **Physical controls:** Ensuring assets such as inventory and cash are safe.

The types of control activity that should be used in an accounting system to address systemic weaknesses can be remembered using the mnemonic **SPAMSOAP**:

(a) Segregation of duties – eg different members of staff should (1) open the post, (2) record cheques received and (3) bank cheques received. These can be built into integrated computer systems, eg an invoice is raised by one user, but a manager must log in to approve them. Others may be manual, such as proof of authorisation by a signature on a hard copy report.

(b) Physical controls – controls over the physical security of accounting records and assets such as cash and inventory, eg lock cash receipts in a safe until they are banked; require codes to unlock the cash tills; lock the stores where inventory is kept.

(c) **A**uthorisation controls

> **Authorisation and approval of transactions:** Undertaken by supervisors and managers – this shows the person processing the transaction that it is valid, eg overtime should be approved by departmental heads.
>
> **Authorisation controls:** These ensure that only authorised personnel can make changes, such as to standing data or to authorise a bank payment.

(d) **M**anagement controls – managers should review whether activity controls are being carried out within the accounting system, eg comparing budget to actual performance in a budgetary control report, and comparing performance and position from one period to the next using ratio analysis.

(e) **S**upervision controls – there should be close oversight of people performing accounting tasks day to day.

Reviews: Performed by supervisors or managers by looking at summaries and reports of transactions, eg to ensure they are reasonable.

(f) **O**rganisation – the way tasks and the business as a whole are organised should support internal control eg clear lines of responsibility, delegation and reporting, and adequate resources being available for the accounting system.

(g) **A**rithmetic and accounting controls – checks on whether transactions have been processed accurately and completely eg **reconciliations** such as a bank statement and a cash book, or a payables ledger account and a statement from the supplier, can also highlight if errors have occurred

Accounting controls: Controls which help to identify mistakes in the accounting records.

Other accounting controls can be highlighted by a trial balance being out of balance or a computer system not allowing a journal to be posted where the debits do not equal the credits.

Reconciliations: Checks where staff ensure that two different sources of information agree or that any differences are understood, eg bank reconciliations verifying the bank statement to the bank account on the nominal ledger.

(h) **P**ersonnel controls – appropriately recruited, selected and trained accounting staff should be employed

Activity 1: The control environment

Consider the following scenario at CCC which occurred in September 20X2:

Stefan was the first to arrive at work on Monday morning. He opened the post, and began logging cheques received into the day book when the telephone rang. It was Margaret to say that she had an emergency dental appointment for that morning, so she would be late for work. Stefan went back to his task of processing the mail; without noticing he had dropped a cheque behind the desk, before he had written it into the day book. Stefan put the day book, with the cheques inside, onto his desk whilst he went to discuss the morning's deliveries with the warehouse manager.

Paula Cookridge popped into the office before she joined her husband, John, for lunch. As she was short on cash and did not have time to go to the bank, she helped herself to £40 from the petty cash tin, and told Stefan that John would replace it this afternoon when he returned from their lunch date.

Paul Collins asked when Pritpal, one of the fitters, would be at work as he needed some rolls of vinyl to be moved into the warehouse from the pallet delivery outside. Pritpal is certified in counter-balance forklift truck operation. In Pritpal's absence Jake Brew offered to move the vinyl as he has been shown how to use the forklift by Pritpal on a number of occasions. Paul accepts his offer as Pritpal is delayed in traffic.

John was concerned that some customers were becoming increasingly slow in making payments on their credit accounts. He asked Stefan to prepare a schedule of receivables, but Stefan was busy drawing up the sales invoices (he uses his Word template and manually inputs details from the sales team) and asked if this could be done next month. Stefan had not chased up late payments recently because he was too busy. Constructing a receivables ledger from the word document invoices took at least two to three hours, and there was a lot of post still to be processed that morning.

Sonja, who had been on holiday, was approached by Ron Sellers, one of the sales team. He had been expecting commission totalling £800 in his wages, but Margaret (who had covered for Sonja last month) had not processed this and had only prepared his wages based on Ron's basic hours worked. Ron told Sonja that he really needed this money, but Sonja, knowing she could do nothing until the next wages run, told Ron he would have to wait seven days.

Ron was so upset by this news that Sonja was consumed with guilt, and she told Ron that she would borrow the money out of the petty cash tin and replace it when she made his wages up next week.

Margaret keeps the company cheque book in her drawer, but as she only works part time, the drawer is often left unlocked.

Required

Highlight areas of weakness from the extract above relating to CCC.

4 Security of the accounting system

The accounting system must be secure so that it can perform its function. This can be done in a number of ways, for instance preventing initial access to the system with a physical barrier (locks on the doors) or using passwords to prevent unauthorised access to the software.

Physical controls: Ensure assets such as inventory and cash are safe.

Information processing controls: Controls relating to the transactions and standing data in the computerised accounting system.

Integrity controls: To verify and validate input data, the processing of data and the production of reports.

4.1 Limiting access

Security controls: Controls in the accounting system that cover integrity controls, system controls and physical access controls.

All users of a computerised accounting system should have a password that gives them access to the parts of the system they are authorised to use. This ensures staff cannot complete operations that are not related to their role eg access to payroll systems will be strictly limited to HR staff.

Management should guard against malicious or fraudulent access using a variety of **security controls,** such as physical barriers (locks on doors and cabinets), deterrents (alarm system or security), IT controls (passwords, firewalls and ensuring adequate disaster recovery processes are in place, such as backups of data) and monitoring of controls (management reviews, authorisation requirements etc).

Such controls in the accounting system include implementing **integrity controls**.

There should be **information processing controls** over standing data to ensure only authorised changes are made; for example, new suppliers can only be entered onto a system by an authorised person, or payroll data only accessible by payroll staff.

Ensuring strict segregation of duties by reducing the number of people involved in different parts of each process and minimising the opportunity for fraud and error will help to ensure the integrity of standing data and ensuring only authorised transactions are made.

> **Integrity of data:** Ensures that data is complete, secure and accurate.

4.2 Preventing errors

The accounting system should have robust integrity controls to verify and validate input data, the processing of data and the production of reports.

These should include input controls on completeness of data input to the system (eg batch processing, total checks, not allowing journals to be posted which do not balance). There can also be programme controls ensuring the accuracy of data input to the system, such as an automatic check on the calculation of VAT. Some controls, such as integrity controls, check the consistency and validity of the data being entered eg the correct format of figures are used (eg allowing invoice numbers in the correct format, AA12345) and checking the calculation of VAT. They are rules in the system which allow only certain types of data to be inserted.

> **Processing controls:** May be used to warn the user if they try to log out before processing is finished or close a document prior to saving. Data is also checked for arithmetical accuracy.

Processing controls verify the data validation and editing procedures. They can also ensure that forms are not closed without being saved or can only be altered by one user at a time. They also used for ensuring arithmetical accuracy or completeness of data. One example of this is 'batch invoice processing' whereby the total value of the invoices is independently calculated and then the total of the invoices entered onto the system is verified against this total.

Activity 2: Security and IT at CCC

Below is an extract from the CCC IT policy currently in place.

> All computers can only be accessed by staff who have been authorised by management to use CCC's computers. All computers must be password protected.
>
> Computers must only be loaded with licensed software owned by the company. No changes to software are permitted without the consent of CCC's directors. No member of staff is allowed to load any software onto computers without prior permission from the management.
>
> No unauthorised devices are to be used for saving, uploading or downloading work (eg discs, memory sticks, external hard drives or other devices) other than those purchased and approved by the company.
>
> Computers should only be used for company business and must not be used to access any social networking sites.
>
> Using the information available in the pre-seen information on CCC, comment on the following:

Required

(a) What rules should be put in place regarding the use of and control of passwords at CCC?

(b) Why are these important?

(c) Note any other issues regarding the current security of the accounting system and IT practice at CCC.

---

5 Internal control systems for different types of organisations

As regulation and reporting requirements become more complex, the underlying system of internal controls must also be reviewed and assessed for suitability by management.

The level of complexity and size of the system of internal controls will depend on the size and nature of the organisation.

Large companies produce significant amounts of data which is usually recorded electronically. Therefore, large companies usually need a mixture of controls over electronic data as well as some manual internal controls. Large companies usually have lots of staff which makes segregation of duties easier.

A **small or medium-sized company** may have fewer staff members to perform controls and therefore they are less able to implement segregation of duty. These companies might use simpler accounting systems with more manual controls.

Businesses that are **cash-based** but have good physical controls over cash and regular reconciliations to ensure that the cash balances are correct, for example reconciling the cash register balance at the end of the day. A cash-based business is usually considered to be riskier than a business that operates on credit.

Credit-based businesses tend to have a lot more documentation at each stage of their transaction cycles. This paper (or electronic) documentation makes it easier to establish an audit trail to implement internal controls and monitor whether they have been adhered to.

Online businesses will need different controls to physical businesses. As well as strong controls over the IT systems, there will need to be good physical controls over any inventory, especially as these businesses often have higher levels of returns.

6 Ethical behaviour within an organisation

In previous chapters, we discussed the impact of the organisation's size, culture and type on its accounting function. Here we consider how ethical principles should guide the practices and controls within an accounting system. In the Level 3 unit *Business Awareness* you learned the five fundamental principles of professional ethics within the AAT *Code of Professional Ethics* (the AAT Code).

Integrity: Being straightforward and honest in all professional and business relationships.

Objectivity: Not allowing bias, conflict of interest or undue influence of others to override professional or business relationships.

Professional competence and due care: Having the right level of current professional knowledge and skill to give competent professional service, and acting diligently and in accordance with applicable and professional standards.

Confidentiality: Not disclosing confidential information except in appropriate circumstances, and not profiting from confidential information.

Professional behaviour: Complying with relevant laws and regulations and not bringing disrepute on the accounting profession.

(AAT, 2017)

Management should ensure that these principles are embedded within the organisation's accounting system.

Assessment focus point

Ensure you have a thorough understanding of the five fundamental principles of professional ethics. If you need to revisit these areas, review your Level 3 *Business Awareness* Course Book for more details.

6.1 Fundamental principles of professional ethics

Ethics: A set of generally accepted principles that guide behaviour.

Ethical values: Assumptions and beliefs about what constitutes 'right' and 'wrong' behaviour.

Fundamental principles of professional ethics: The principles that underpin how a professional accountant should behave.

Individuals hold ethical values, often reflecting the beliefs of the families, cultures and educational environments in which they grew up.

Companies should also have ethical values, based on the norms and standards of behaviour that their leaders believe will best help them express their identity and achieve their objectives. The values of the company are usually set out in its mission statement.

Companies, just like individuals, are members of society and are therefore responsible for their actions, and can be held accountable for the effects of those actions eg companies can be convicted of crimes such as manslaughter, just like people.

Therefore, companies should behave ethically towards their stakeholders.

6.2 Ensuring ethical practice within the system

Management and directors need to ensure that ethical practice is maintained within their organisation. Often there will be an organisational policy or mission statement, or a code of conduct that employees are expected to follow.

Activity 3: Ensuring ethical behaviour at work

CCC has recently revised its website, adding information regarding its mission statement (see Chapter 1, Activity 10). Stefan, the Accounts Receivable Clerk, has suggested that the five ethical principles as set out by the AAT *Code of Professional Ethics* be added to the website. The directors have agreed and intend to show how CCC's accounting function (and all other staff) achieves these principles in order to demonstrate what an ethical organisation it is in practice.

Required

Using the table below, identify how CCC can ensure its accounting function (and all other staff) uphold the ethical standards demanded by the AAT *Code of Professional* Ethics.

Fundamental ethical principle	Explain how CCC may demonstrate these principles in practice
Integrity	
Objectivity	
Professional competence and due care	
Confidentiality	
Professional behaviour	

6.3 Ethical risks to the system

The accounting function (Chapter 1) plays an important role in establishing and maintaining the ethical culture within an organisation. Risks to ethical behaviour may come in a variety of forms:

- Criminal behaviour (bribery, money laundering, theft)
- Non-compliance with organisational policy or regulations (data protection, AAT Code)
- Bullying or intimidating behaviour
- Poor decision making (short-term decision making, reputational risks, environmental hazards)

Let us consider some ethical issues concerning CCC's accounting function in line with these fundamental principles.

Activity 4: Ethics conflict at CCC

Consider the following scenarios:

(1) Stefan is asked to produce an aged receivables listing for John Cookridge as at 30 April 20X3. However, he does not have up to date figures because cash received has not yet been allocated to customers, and Stefan knows that the aged receivables report will look worse than the underlying situation. Sonja suggests that to get the report done in time he should use averages for the missing figures.

(2) Margaret has opened a letter from an estate agent requesting financial information about one of CCC's customers, who is applying to rent a property. The information is needed as soon as possible, by email, in order to secure approval for the rent agreement.

(3) A friend tells Stefan on a night out that she expects to inherit money from a recently deceased uncle. She asks him how she will be affected by inheritance tax, capital gains tax and other matters.

(4) A supplier is so pleased with how promptly Stefan paid her that she offers him a free weekend break in a luxury hotel, just as a 'thank you'.

Required

Identify the ethical issues at risk in the scenarios and recommend a course of action to be taken by Stefan or Margaret in each case.

7 What is fraud?

You were introduced to the concept of fraud and the regulations surrounding it during the Level 3 *Business Awareness* module. It is useful to review the key points before attempting the activities in this section.

> **Fraud:** A crime in which the criminal **intentionally** makes a gain or causes a loss to another person by depriving them of assets.

Legally, there are three types of fraud (Fraud Act 2006: s.1):

- False representation
- Failure to disclose information
- Abuse of position

With respect to the accounting system, the types of fraud which are important are:

Misappropriation of assets: Theft, teeming and lading, payment of false employees or suppliers.

Misstatement of the financial statements: The overstatement of assets or profit, or the understatement of profit, losses or liabilities.

An accounting system is more open to fraud if it contains systemic weaknesses, making it easy to misappropriate assets, or misstate financial information.

Examples of fraud include, but are not restricted to:

- Falsifying financial statements or documents, such as invoices
- Incorrect accounting to purposely hide debts or overstate profits
- False claims about the products being sold by the company (for example, Silicon Valley start-up Theranos)
- Payment fraud, including teeming and lading (misallocation of cash payments)
- Tax evasion, such as understatement of VAT, PAYE or corporate tax.
- Money laundering
- Insider trading
- Embezzlement (fraud by employees in positions of power or trust within a business), such as by creating fictitious suppliers or employees

Activity 5: Potential frauds at CCC

Using the information obtained about CCC from the pre-seen information and any existing knowledge about CCC, consider the key areas where fraud may occur within the business.

Required

Identify the possible frauds that could occur within CCC – even if the controls currently in place make such a fraud unlikely.

	Potential fraud
Purchases and inventory system	
Payroll system	
Bank and cash system	
Sales and aged receivables system	

8 Impact of fraud

Fraud has the following types of impact on a company:

(a) **Financial** – loss of funds or other assets. This in turn affects the company's profitability and the owner's investment in it. It can also affect the company's share price.

(b) **Reputation** – exposure to fraud can affect the company's reputation in the eyes of internal and external stakeholders. This in turn could lead to a loss of business.

(c) **Employee morale** – the trust of existing employees could be damaged. Future recruitment and retention of staff might also be affected.

The following examples illustrate the financial and reputational impacts upon companies which have been fined for financial misstatement, or not having sufficient fraud prevention controls in place:

Real life example: Tesco Stores

In March 2017, Tesco Stores was fined £129 million by the Serious Fraud Office (SFO) and ordered to set up an £85 million compensatory scheme for shareholders and bondholders who bought shares between the results announcement and the accounting misstatement being made public. Tesco settled out of court regarding charges of false accounting and misstatement of profits.

The impact on the company was a £214 million cash outflow, not including legal costs, with Tesco recording an exceptional charge of £235 million for the 2016/2017 accounting year end.

(Reuters, 2017)

Real life example: Rolls-Royce PLC

Rolls-Royce PLC was fined £497.5 million by the SFO in January 2017 in respect of 12 counts of conspiracy to corrupt, false accounting and failure to prevent bribery over a period of 30 years. In addition, the company was fined $170 million by to the US Department of Justice and $25 million by the Brazilian authorities.

(SFO, 2017)

Real life example: Standard Chartered Bank

The Financial Conduct Authority (FCA) fined the bank £102.2 million for failing to maintain adequate anti-money laundering controls between November 2010 and January 2013.

(FCA, 2019)

8.1 What can cause fraud to occur?

Cressey (1973) explained that fraud was likely to occur if three conditions were present:

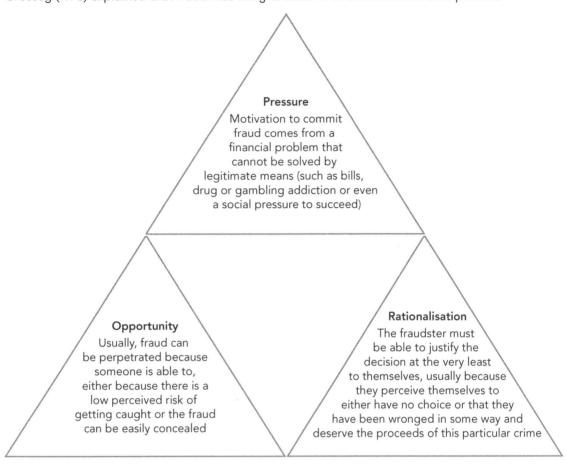

Pressure
Motivation to commit fraud comes from a financial problem that cannot be solved by legitimate means (such as bills, drug or gambling addiction or even a social pressure to succeed)

Opportunity
Usually, fraud can be perpetrated because someone is able to, either because there is a low perceived risk of getting caught or the fraud can be easily concealed

Rationalisation
The fraudster must be able to justify the decision at the very least to themselves, usually because they perceive themselves to either have no choice or that they have been wronged in some way and deserve the proceeds of this particular crime

Knowing that fraud is usually a product of these three conditions means that an organisation can focus on each one when considering both **prevention** and **detection** of fraud. For example:

- **Pressure** – are staff likely to be affected by external factors, such as blackmail, addiction or extortion?
- **Opportunity** – are assets likely to be vulnerable (and are any of our internal controls poor)?
- **Rationalisation** – are staff disenfranchised or desperate enough to commit fraud, and do our recruitment procedures always check employee references for any previous fraudulent behaviour?

Having a better understanding of the conditions that need to be present for fraud to occur can help an organisation design **suitable controls** that can attempt to **address** such conditions. The fraud triangle is a good way of understanding these conditions.

9 Controls to prevent fraud and systemic weaknesses

In this section, we look specifically at the types of fraud which can occur within the business and, using the scenario of CCC, identify potential issues and consider the impact on CCC.

The management of a company have a duty to put in place adequate controls to safeguard the company and its assets. You have seen many of the safeguarding controls in the Level 3 *Business Awareness* module and have also covered them earlier in this chapter (SPAMSOAP).

The main types of controls which can help prevent fraud include controls for the accounting system can be grouped into the following categories:

- **Staff controls** – segregation of duties
- **Management controls** – review of controls and regular checks on control activities
- **Physical controls** – locking away confidential files and ensuring office security

- **Information processing and generalIT controls** – password protection, access limitations and integration of systems

> **Fraud controls:** Internal controls specifically against fraud in the areas of staff controls, management controls, physical controls and IT controls.

9.1 Sales system fraud

Fraud within the sales system is possible because the system involves the receipt of money, and this risk is more severe where this is in the form of cash, such as a shop.

Activity 6: Sales system fraud

The following is some further information given about an event in January 20X3 at CCC. Use this additional information and any existing knowledge about CCC to formulate your answer.

> Stefan was tidying up in the office one evening and was surprised to discover two cheques behind a desk. One was dated August 20X2, and one November 20X2. He put them in the in-tray intending to bank them the next day.
>
> John Cookridge asked for a copy of the aged receivables report, as he hadn't seen one for nearly four months. He was annoyed when he discovered that one of the credit accounts, opened for B. Braithwaite, had made no payments against credit given at all so far. This customer had bought £1,000 worth of goods and paid an initial deposit in July 20X2 but had made no payment since then. He asked Stefan to track back through the account and Stefan realised that no credit reference agency had been used to vet the customer before accepting their initial order, so he decided to contact the agency to check on this customer, only to find that he had a very poor credit score.
>
> Meanwhile John continued to review the aged receivables report and discovered that not only had debts been written off without his knowledge but also that over 50% of the invoices over 60 days old had no payments allocated against them. Unallocated cash amounted to £5,645.
>
> Stefan advised that there had been a large debt of £2,300 written off the previous month, as it dated back to the previous October. Stefan said that although he had tried to chase the debt, the telephone number rang out, and the customer had taken the flooring with him (so no delivery address had been logged by the sales staff).
>
> When John came to lock up the business at the end of Thursday, he discovered that the tills on the shop floor had not been emptied or reconciled to the day's takings.

Required

(a) **Identify the types of fraud which could occur in the sales system at CCC based on the information you have been given in this extract. Also explain why you think this fraud risk has arisen.**

Fraud which could occur at CCC	Why this risk has arisen

Fraud which could occur at CCC	Why this risk has arisen

(b) Consider the financial and non-financial impacts these frauds could have on CCC.

9.2 Purchases system fraud

Fraud within the purchases system is possible because the system includes the ability to order goods from suppliers and then to make payments.

One of the general controls in place to prevent such examples of fraud is segregation of duties: same member of the accounting team should not be allowed to place orders with suppliers, book in goods received, and then process payments to them.

BPP

Activity 7: Purchases system fraud

The following events happened at CCC during March 20X3:

Margaret needed to place a stationery order for CCC. She asked the staff what they needed and placed the order, including some additional paper for her nephew who is studying at university.

CarPet Suppliers, one of CCC's major suppliers, has requested urgent payment of an invoice that has been outstanding for 60 days. This invoice is for £15,000 and, though this would normally have been paid, there were not enough funds in the bank to cover this amount.

When Margaret informed John of this, he was very surprised at the size of the invoice and asked her to review all the GRNs for October to see what carpets had been ordered to cause such a large invoice. Margaret spent a day completing this reconciliation and found that there was an error and they had been charged for 1,000 metres of twisted Wilton instead of 100, this having a wholesale price of £15.00 per metre including VAT.

When John was checking the invoice, he asked Margaret to produce a report of outstanding invoices and discovered some new suppliers with long outstanding debts which he did not recognise.

Required

Identify the risks from the control weaknesses in the above extract and make any recommendations to improve the controls.

Ensure your answer is specific to the scenario.

10 Detecting fraud

Internal controls within the accounting system should be designed not only to address weaknesses and prevent fraud and errors, but also to help detect when they have occurred.

The key controls that detect whether fraud or errors have occurred are:

(a) **Spot checks** on whether control activities have taken place
(b) **Performance reviews** and comparisons, using:
    (i)   The **budgetary control report**: compare actual results to budgeted results

(ii) **Ratio analysis:** compare this period to the previous period, and evaluate the relationships between figures in the financial statements (eg level of receivables compared with level of sales)

(c) **Reconciliation** of information produced by the accounting system with external evidence, such as bank statements and supplier statements

(d) **Control accountreconciliations** where transactions are recorded in individual accounts and in total (eg receivables and payables)

Management can use financial information to analyse and review the controls of an organisation. Financial information can highlight issues such as potential inefficiencies as well as possible fraudulent behaviour, eg decreases in profit margin may suggest that costs are being poorly managed, or may highlight an issue such as theft of inventory.

10.1 Management accounts

Management reports can be structured to ensure that the most useful information is available to the user of the report. The information may be summarised into a form of profit or loss statement, or include additional information such as variance analysis, aged receivables analysis or capital expenditure review for the period.

Ideally, these reports should be consistently prepared and monitored on a regular basis, eg monthly, so as to highlight any significant issues arising, and to prompt investigations and corrective action where required.

Activity 8: Detecting fraud using financial information

The following are some extracts from the management accounts which were completed at the year end for CCC. Use these and the financial statements in the pre-seen scenario for this activity. CCC completes quarterly management accounts only.

Extracts from the management accounts for CCC Ltd as at 31 December 20X2

	20X2		20X1	
	Carpets	Vinyl	Carpets	Vinyl
	£000	£000	£000	£000
Revenue	379	727	425	505
Cost of sales	(287)	(416)	(282)	(351)
Gross margin	92	311	143	154

	All products		All products	
	£000	£000	£000	£000
Rent and rates	30		30	
Salaries: administration and management	87		87	
Salaries: sales	105		60	
Salaries: directors	120		110	
Motor expenses	19		10	
Irrecoverable debts	22		8	
Finance costs	5		6	

	All products		All products	
	£000	£000	£000	£000
Other costs	13		10	
Total costs		401		321
Net profit/(loss)		2		(24)

Required

Using the knowledge you have obtained from the earlier activities, review the management accounts above and highlight areas which present potential issues for the company, making any recommendations you believe are appropriate.

Note. There is no requirement to calculate ratios.

Chapter summary

- Internal controls in the accounting system aim: to protect it from systemic weaknesses; avoid fraudulent activities and human error; ensure compliance with applicable laws and regulations; and ensure the company is working to meet its objectives.
- The system of internal controls consists of an effective control environment; the entity's risk assessment process; the entity's process to monitor the system of internal control; the information system and communication; and control activities.
- Control activities in an accounting system address systemic weaknesses and control risks.
- Control activities consist of segregation of duties; physical controls; authorisation and approval of transactions; management controls; supervision controls; organisational controls; arithmetic and accounting controls; and personnel controls. The SPAMSOAP mnemonic may help you remember these.
- Information processing controls affect transactions and consist of input controls, accuracy controls, authorisation checks, processing controls and controls over standing data.
- General IT controls protect the general computer environment.
- The limitations of controls include people making mistakes, where controls may not be operated effectively or where people may deliberately circumvent controls.
- For each control objective within a system, the risks controlled and control activities need to be identified.
- Within any of the systems, segregation of duties – as far as it is possible given the size of the accounting function and the number of its staff – is a vital control.
- In the credit sales system, control objectives etc are identified for: taking orders and extending credit; dispatching and invoicing goods; recording and accounting for sales and returns; and receiving payment.
- In the purchases system, control objectives etc are identified for: ordering; receipt of goods and services; accounting; and payments.
- In the payroll system, control objectives etc are identified for: setting wages and salaries; recording; payments; and deductions.

Activity answers

Activity 1: The control environment

Within CCC, controls are very informal. Reliance is often based on trust. Formal internal controls would support the accounting system and reduce the possibility of fraud occurring.

Petty cash – no control system is in place. People can help themselves to cash as and when needed; there is no control or reconciliation at the end of each day. Paula is no longer an employee and is still able to help herself to petty cash.

Cheques received in the post are not secured away in a locked drawer or a safe prior to sending to the bank.

Minimal segregation of duties – Stefan opens the post alone and logs the cheques into the day book without any checks or verifications in place.

Payroll controls are weak in that Sonja was able to make additional payments to Ron without any authorisation. She also did not verify the payment prior to making it in cash to Ron. There is also the potential that this was not documented, and there is no evidence Ron signed for the additional monies paid to him.

Health and safety regulations are not adhered to – an untrained person using a forklift without having the relevant training. This may be an issue if there was an accident as it is likely that CCC's insurance will be invalid.

The accounts receivable system is manual and there has been no regular review by management of the debt recovery process.

The company cheque book is not stored securely in a locked drawer or safe and so there is risk that it might be used inappropriately.

Activity 2: Security and IT at CCC

(a) The company might put in place the following rules regarding the use and control of passwords:

- Passwords must not be written down.
- Passwords must not be shared.
- Passwords must be changed regularly.
- Passwords must not be generic.
- When a staff member leaves the company, password access must be cancelled that day.
- Password access can only be set up for new staff with management authorisation.
- Staff access to different parts of the system must be regularly reviewed.

(b) These rules and controls protect the integrity of the system and the company. If one password is used by all staff (generic), there is little point in using them as the whole system is open to all. This lack of control then increases the risk of errors, from staff using parts of the system they are not trained to use, and fraud.

Access to the system should be controlled so that staff are not granted access to parts they do not require. If staff leave their access should be cancelled immediately so they cannot continue to use the system, and other staff cannot use their passwords. Often companies make sharing of passwords a disciplinary offence to ensure that controls are maintained.

(c) The policy states that only licensed software purchased by the company may be installed on company devices; however, the warehouse has two computers which have a personal version of software on them supplied by the warehouse manager.

There is no evidence of the payroll and purchase systems being regularly backed up, either to local backup devices or 'cloud' based support. It is not stated whether Stefan is using company-purchased hardware for the backup of the sales system or not. It is not evident that this is kept off site or locked away in the company safe in case of theft or fire.

Doors to the accounting department are kept open (even though there is a secure keypad-based lock) and the public can easily enter as the bathrooms are nearby.

Payroll is prepared in the same open area as the rest of the accounting function. There is a risk that secure and confidential information regarding staff salaries is open to access by other employees.

Activity 3: Ensuring ethical behaviour at work

Fundamental ethical principle	Explain how CCC may demonstrate these principles in practice
Integrity	The accounting function and system should be used to ensure information is accurate and not misleading. Staff should ensure that any issues regarding quality of data are raised immediately with management. The directors should ensure that financial statements are completed in a timely fashion.
Objectivity	Staff must not allow bias, conflict of interest or undue influence of others to override professional or business relationships.
Professional competence and due care	Ensure employees regularly update their technical knowledge, especially those with a responsibility for payroll, taxes and financial record keeping. Ensure regular monitoring of controls and processes by management and make adjustments when the business needs it or the organisation changes. Ensure all employees are aware of the health and safety regulations at work and that they attend any relevant courses. If staff do not feel that they can adequately complete a task, or are asked to do something which they do not feel able to do, then the issue should be raised with management and either an alternative resource should be found or training should be supplied.
Confidentiality	Security of payroll, supplier and customer data should be enhanced. Company business should not be discussed outside of the office or with third parties. Passwords should be used and data should be kept secured in locked cabinets and security of information at all times.
Professional behaviour	Ensure staff remain professional and courteous to customers and suppliers and other employees. A culture should be built that enables staff to supply accurate and timely information to the best of their abilities.

Activity 4: Ethics conflict at CCC

(1) There is an **integrity** issue here alongside a **professional competence and due care** issue. Using averages instead of actual figures will almost certainly result in an inaccurate listing, and a report prepared without 'due care'.

Stefan should report the problem to Mr Cookridge and ask for an extension to the deadline in order to provide an accurate listing.

(2) There is a **confidentiality** issue here. Margaret needs the customer's authority to disclose the information; she may also need to confirm the identity of the person making the request. She should also take steps to protect the security of the information when she sends it; for

example, not using email (which can be intercepted), and stating clearly that the information is confidential.

There is also a **professional behaviour** issue: to comply with the Data Protection Regulations, it is likely that CCC has rules about what to do on receipt of such a request.

Margaret should not divulge any information without checking with a manager that she is legally allowed to do so.

(3) There are issues of **professional competence and due care** here. Stefan is not qualified to give advice on matters of taxation. Even if he were qualified, any answer he gives on the spot would risk being incomplete or inaccurate causing his friend tax losses. Stefan should advise his friend that he is unable to help, and point him in the direction of a qualified tax accountant.

(4) There is an **objectivity** issue here as the gift is of significant value. Think about how it looks: a third-party observer is entitled to wonder what 'special favours' deserve this extra reward – and/or how such a gift may bias Stefan when making payments to the supplier in future. Stefan should politely decline the offer, pointing out that he is merely doing his job.

Activity 5: Potential frauds at CCC

Frauds that could occur within the accounting system could include the following (note that this list is not exhaustive):

	Potential fraud
Purchases and inventory system	• Theft of assets – computers or other assets could be stolen by any of the staff within CCC due to the easy access to the accounts office.
	• Theft of inventory – there is no mention of controls such as inventory counts to prevent the theft of inventory from the warehouse. The Excel spreadsheet used to record movements of, or changes to, the level of inventory is also an ineffective control as staff fail to update it.
	• Overpayment of supplier invoices – there is no control to verify that cheques prepared to pay suppliers equate to the amount owed and invoiced.
Payroll system	• Overstatement of wages – there are no controls in place to approve actual wages paid to staff, so the Sonja, Wages Clerk, could overstate wages by either overpaying on hours worked and/or the hourly rate.
	• Overstatement of hours worked – the stores supervisor could add more hours to the staff rotas than physically worked by staff.
	• Monetary theft via the setting up of a ghost employee – there are no controls over the addition of new starters to the payroll system, such as a requirement for documentation that cannot be overridden, segregation of duties, or linking to HR records. This means that a person could set up a fictional employee and keep the wages 'earned' for themselves.

	Potential fraud
Bank and cash system	• Theft of cheques – there are few controls in place to store the cheque book securely, and it is stored in a drawer which is not always locked.
	• Theft of cash from the office – petty cash is kept in the staff room and there is little control over access to the office. There is no one member of staff responsible for the petty cash tin and the only control is a sheet on which any expenses paid for using petty cash should be logged. However, this control is currently ineffective as it would appear that it is not being used. Staff have also been borrowing money from this tin on occasions. There are frequently discrepancies between the amount that should be in the tin and surprise at finding the tin empty or running low.
	• Theft of cheques from the mail – no separate controls are in place to record cheques received.
	• Theft of cash and/or cheques from tills – the tills are not balanced each evening so there is no accountability for any missing cash and/or cheques.
Sales and aged receivables system	• Under-recording of goods sold – there are few controls in place to ensure goods sold are accurately recorded.
	• Writing off debts – there are no controls to ensure that debts from customers are not written off, or to ensure that they are written off when they should be.

Activity 6: Sales system fraud

(a)

Fraud which could occur at CCC	Why this risk has arisen
Stolen cash receipts through the non-reconciliation of the till records and the cash inside them	The risk is increased by leaving the tills full of cash overnight. Any error or shortfall will not be detected until the next day or when the staff come to reconcile the takings. Having significant amounts of cash on the premises increases the threat of theft or loss.
No credit check undertaken against B. Braithwaite	This is a potential fraud risk as the customer may buy items on credit with no intention of paying (theft of inventory) or the customer may be a fictitious one set up by an unscrupulous member of the sales team who wants to inflate their sales figures for commission payments.
Unallocated cash	Unallocated cash is a fraud risk. There is a risk that sales staff could have diverted funds from a customer and are using more recent cash receipts to try to cover this up, but there will always be a difference if the invoiced amounts do not match.
Writing off debts	All debts require management authorisation to be written off. Currently, debts are written off as and when Stefan believes that they cannot be collected or they have got 'just too old'.

(b) Without management or senior staff performing regular reviews of the aged receivables report, the following issues may occur:

Financial loss

The unallocated cash does not show what debts or final balances need to be settled by customers. By delaying the allocation of cash, it is possible that fraud could occur by 'teeming and lading' (cash receipts being skimmed off and then applying other customer receipts to cover it. By delaying the overall outstanding debt, this type of fraud may only appear if another person performs a reconciliation of the ledger or the customers are contacted directly).

Financial loss due to staff inflating the sales figures and earning more commission.

Financial loss due to inflated sales and risk of overstating VAT liability.

Non-financial

The high level of unallocated cash suggests that customers' invoices may appear to be outstanding when they have in fact been paid. This could adversely affect customer relations if they are chased for debts that they have settled in full.

Equally, with the cheques being dropped and lost when they are received in the post, the risk of paid debts being chased will affect customer relations.

If fraud has occurred, staff morale may drop due to a climate of suspicion.

Activity 7: Purchases system fraud

Ordering goods for own use – there are issues around segregation of duties between ordering, booking goods into inventory and making payments, plus appropriate authorisations. Management should authorise all purchase orders, so that all orders placed can be verified and there are no 'surprises' in value or in finding that staff are using company funds to purchase goods for personal use.

The potential for fictitious suppliers – there should be management authorisation of all new suppliers added to the system; reconciliation of payments to invoices; and some segregation of duties for these processes. The new suppliers may all be valid, but management should also be reviewing whether they represent best value in terms of price, quality and credit terms offered.

Invoices incorrectly calculated – CCC may have paid the incorrect amount of £15,000 if this had not been such a significant error and investigated further. Suitable controls would be to match goods received to purchases orders, then matching the invoice to the purchase order when it arrives to check that the supplier has correctly calculated the quantities and prices.

Time wasted – it took Margaret all day to reconcile the manual system to find out what had happened with the incorrectly calculated invoice. If there was a fully integrated system, this would have been highlighted much sooner and any investigation would have taken significantly less time.

By delaying the payment to the supplier, and not raising the issue earlier, CCC has risked affecting the relationship with this supplier.

Cash flow effect – working capital would have been significantly affected if this £15,000 invoice had been paid, and there is the potential for strained relations with the bank if CCC had asked for an extension to its bank overdraft. Any request to increase the overdraft will result in higher interest charges, as well as possible arrangement fees.

Activity 8: Detecting fraud using financial information

- **Irrecoverable debts** – have increased by 175% (whereas revenue has increased by 19%). This suggests that there may be issues regarding the collection of cash or screening of customers (from Activity 6 we know B. Braithwaite was added with no credit checks). However, from a detection of fraud basis, this could also suggest that cash is being collected from customers and these debts are being written off rather than the cash being applied to them (there was lots of unallocated cash in the most recent aged receivables report). Irrecoverable debts which are written off should also be authorised by a member of management. Management should review a list of the debts (one of the directors last looked at it four months ago) to be written off with explanations as to why this is the case and steps taken to recover any outstanding debt.

- **Sales staff salaries** – have increased by 75% which, given the rise of revenue by 19%, is odd. There had been a case of one of the sales staff requesting additional commission and this being paid without being checked. This is a potential area of fraud. Sales commission should be reviewed by the directors prior to being paid. Management should be able to review the sales made by the member of staff (including any credits or refunds given). In order to ensure that credit notes are not being raised after the invoice in order to 'boost' sales, the commission should only be paid after a predetermined period of time (eg quarterly intervals) to allow cut-off testing to be performed.

- **Other costs** – management should ensure they understand what drives these costs so that they do not simply 'creep up' over time, as many of these should be fixed in nature.

- **Other factors which may be considered**

  - Ensuring that the management accounts are regularly reviewed by the management team

  - Monthly management accounts rather than quarterly would help to highlight any problems most quickly

  - Looking at the actual results against budget to see if the company is 'on track' and the accounts look reasonable

Test your learning

1 What type of control activity is each of the following actions? Write your answer in the space provided.

Action	Type of control activity
Person A matches dispatch notes to invoices; Person B creates invoice to customer	
Control account reconciliation	
Petty cash box kept locked	
Adequate resourcing of accounting function	
Review of budgetary control report	

2 Identify for each of the following control activities which type of security control they are an example of.

Activities	Type of security control
Validation of input data	▼
Passwords	▼
Archiving	▼

Picklist
- Integrity control
- Management control
- Physical access control
- Segregation of duties
- System control

3 Complete the following statement:

Management should regularly ensure that staff perform [▼] of the receivables

ledger to ensure accuracy and completeness of the data.

Picklist
- Assessments
- Inspections
- Reconciliations
- Teeming and lading

4 Complete the following statement:

Control objectives in relation to taking orders and extending credit are part of the

[▼] system of the accounting system.

- Payroll
- Purchases
- Sales

5 **Complete the following statement:**

Completion of GRNs is a control activity related to the control objective of [▼] .

Picklist

- Ensuring goods and services received are used for the company's purposes
- Only accepting goods and services that have been ordered and appropriately authorised
- Only accepting goods received that are of a sufficient quantity for the purposes of the organisation
- Recording all money received

6 **Complete the following statement:**

Allocating one customer's payment to another customer's account in order to balance the books

and detract from a shortfall is called [▼] .

Picklist

- Identity fraud
- Inflation
- Reconciliation and review
- Teeming and lading

7 **For each of the following situations where fraud is being discussed, identify the fraud triangle condition that is being described.**

Situation	Fraud triangle condition
'They never check on the older items in the warehouse, so they are the easiest ones to steal.'	▼
'I have worked so hard for this company over the years and yet no-one notices. I am definitely entitled to take items out of the stationery cupboard for my own personal use.'	▼
'If I don't find the money in the next week, my house will be repossessed by the building society. I have to steal cash from the safe because I have no other way of finding the money I owe.'	▼

Picklist

- Dishonesty
- Opportunity
- Pressure
- Rationalisation

 BPP

3   Accounting systems

Learning outcomes

3.1   **An organisation's accounting system and its effectiveness**

Learners need to understand:

3.1.1 control objectives, risks and control procedures for accounting systems:

- purchasing
- sales
- expenses
- payroll
- inventory
- non-current assets
- bank and cash

3.1.2 how an organisation's accounting system can support ethical standards and sustainability practice.

Learners need to be able to:

3.1.3 identify deficiencies in accounting systems that have an impact on:

- cost-effectiveness
- reliability
- timeliness

3.1.4 analyse the cause of deficiencies in accounting systems

3.1.5 evaluate impact of deficiencies in an accounting system including

- time
- money
- reputation.

3.2   **Risk of fraud**

Learners need to understand:

3.2.1 the risk assessment process:

- identify the risk
- evaluate the risk
- respond to the risk (manage/mitigate risk by taking appropriate action)
- ensure compliance (legal and regulatory)
- monitor, review and report.

Learners need to be able to:

3.2.2 assess the impact of poor internal controls on an organisation's exposure to risk

3.2.3 assess risk using the following measures:

- risk matrix
- low, medium, high
- numerical grade (where the number increases as the risk becomes more serious)

3.2.4 recommend a response to risk, ensuring compliance with regulatory and legal requirements

3.2.5 propose monitoring review and report actions in response to an identified risk.

3.3 Operating practice

Learners need to understand:

3.3.1 why accounting systems should be reviewed regularly to ensure they are fit for purpose

3.3.2 that the accounting systems used by an organisation should:

- be cost-effective
- encourage ethical principles and practices
- support sustainability principles and practices
- meet the specific information needs of the organisation

Assessment context

The topics covered in this chapter will be included within a number of tasks in the Internal Accounting Systems and Controls unit assessment.

Qualification context

How the accounting system works, especially the bookkeeping system, is covered at earlier stages of your studies in Level 2 and Level 3, as are the topics of ethics and sustainability.

Business context

The accounting system is operated by the accounting function to produce information for both internal and external stakeholders. Its efficient and cost-effective operation is key to the company's success.

The objective of the accounting system is to provide reliable and timely information in a cost – effective manner. Any accounting system will be subject to a number of controls to prevent and detect errors and potential frauds.

By documenting the system, staff can ensure that they are following the correct procedures, and it will assist when new staff join the organisation and act as a reference guide, especially when tasks are performed infrequently.

Underpinning the accounting system is the adherence to the fundamental values of the AAT *Code of Professional Ethics*.

Every company's accounting system is at risk of fraud and error even if the risks never actually materialise. A company with systemic deficiencies in its accounting system and system of internal controls is particularly at risk. It can lead to serious losses and fines for the company, criminal prosecutions of those responsible, and ultimately the collapse of the company.

Management should assess the risk of fraud and misstatement for each area of the organisation, and here we see how fraud can be graded using a risk matrix, also known as a fraud matrix or fraud risk matrix. This grading gives the management team guidance on areas where they should prioritise their resources. The use of Key Performance Indicators (KPIs) both within the context of the organisation and the industry in which they operate, act as useful tools to highlight potential problems areas.

The definition of fraud, and what it can mean to an organisation is covered, together with the impact of fraud on a business.

Chapter overview

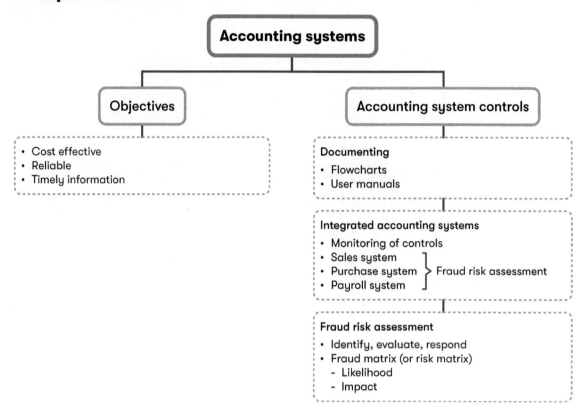

Accounting systems

Objectives
- Cost effective
- Reliable
- Timely information

Accounting system controls

Documenting
- Flowcharts
- User manuals

Integrated accounting systems
- Monitoring of controls
- Sales system ⎤
- Purchase system ⎬ Fraud risk assessment
- Payroll system ⎦

Fraud risk assessment
- Identify, evaluate, respond
- Fraud matrix (or risk matrix)
  - Likelihood
  - Impact

BPP

Introduction

In this chapter, we look at some examples of how accounting systems are structured and consider how they provide information to key stakeholders of the company.

We then consider how to assess whether the accounting systems in place are suitable for the company and whether any improvements could be made to them.

> **Risk:** The threat to the company presented by the control objective not being attained.

Management should revisit their controls on a regular basis, checking that the processes designed are actually in place, and that they are being adhered to. We will see how a **fraud matrix** (also referred to as a risk matrix) can help to evaluate the risks a company faces. We will then look at how to grade the **risk of fraud**.

We also look at the effect that fraud might have on a company, together with the action a company needs to take to **detect** fraudulent behaviour, and what should be done upon the discovery of a fraud.

In this chapter, we also look at the importance of monitoring controls, and why this should be completed on a continual basis.

1 Accounting systems

> **Accounting system:** A system that takes raw data on transactions as its input, processes this, and then produces many outputs to meet the information needs of stakeholders.

Inputs include:

- Raw data from the accounting transactions
- Data from the users, meaning that all users must have training to ensure accurate usage of the system
- Data from management on subjective areas affected by them, such as journals, provisions and aged receivable adjustments

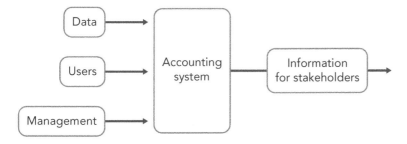

1.1 Objectives of the accounting system

An accounting system is effective if it meets the following objectives:

1.1.1 Cost effectiveness

> **Cost effectiveness:** This ensures that something is good value.

Organisations should consider their needs and the complexity of the information they require. The more complex the system, the more expensive it can be to maintain. The cost of training existing staff and new staff on a new or more complex system should be taken into account.

A **large multinational company** will likely have many locations, about which financial information will be required on a timely basis to ensure control. At each of these locations there are likely to be semi-autonomous departments, each having their own specialisms, for instance inventory control, sales orders, purchasing, and preparation of the local management accounts. In large multinational companies of this type it may be necessary to have a dedicated department to prepare and consolidate the accounts for all the overseas subsidiary companies or branches.

In a **small/medium-sized organisation** each department may require its own manager(s) eg purchase manager and sales manager although, in the small organisations, the lines between these managers may be blurred in order to allow holiday and sickness cover.

A **very small organisation** will want to use a more cost-effective, simpler structure, often requiring managers to take on more than one role eg a single person may be in charge of both the sales and accounting functions. These types of entities will often look to outsource more complex areas of the accountancy function, such as using accountants who will prepare payroll, VAT returns and financial statements on their behalf.

Any changes which are proposed to an accounting system should be carefully considered, weighing up the costs and the benefits of making a change. This is covered in more detail in Chapter 5.

1.1.2 Reliability

> **Reliability:** This ensures a process or system performs consistently well.

The accounting system must operate effectively, processing all transactions accurately and fully, and must be compliant with applicable laws and regulations. The system should allow access to authorised users only, as and when required, and include data security protocols. A modern system will run regular and automated backups of data. Increasingly companies' data is held offsite 'in the cloud' negating the need for daily, manual backups by users onto discs, USB drives or other hardware.

1.1.3 Timeliness

> **Timeliness:** This means that the system should provide information at the required time.

The accounting function and the underlying system needs to be set up in such a way that the reports are accurate and timely. The system will need to provide financial and management information to stakeholders when they require it. It is vital that the system can produce the information required by its users to enable regulatory compliance (such as quarterly VAT returns) and timely reviews of financial performance.

Staff need sufficient training to ensure that they know what information to produce and when it will be required. They also need to have a good understanding of how to use the software to ensure that it is used in an efficient and accurate manner.

Activity 1: CCC accounting system

Use the information provided about the CCC accounting system in the pre-seen information.

Evaluate the following points:

Required

(a) **The cost effectiveness of the CCC accounting system**

(b) **Its reliability**

(c) Do management obtain information in a timely manner?

2 Accounting system controls

It is vital that an organisation has a strong and robust system of internal controls.

All systems in the company must be controlled so that they operate efficiently and effectively. Any potential weaknesses in the system need to be mitigated by controls. These **systemic weaknesses** arise within the accounting system itself, which leave it open to fraud and error.

The accounting system must have built-in controls so that it meets:

- Regulations
- The rules and procedures of the company
- The information requirements of internal and external stakeholders

System controls can include:

- Computer controls (such as passwords or restrictions on staff performing certain operations)
- Manual controls (such as internal audit reviews and supervisory checks)
- Physical controls (such as key pads, locking doors, use of safes and removing cash from tills at night)

These controls were considered in Chapter 2.

2.1 Documenting the system

Systems control starts at the design phase, during which the data flows and processes are mapped. This forms a template for training the users of the system, so that they understand what the system is doing when they are using it. It is vital that these data flows and processes are documented for future reference, in the event that the system breaks down, or needs updating to ensure that it remains fit for purpose. The detailed controls, monitoring and revisions of the accounting system are covered in the following chapters of this Course Book.

2.1.1 Flowcharts

All information systems work by receiving inputs, then processing these into outputs. Each stage of the process can be analysed in detail to draw up a simple system flowchart.

System flowchart: A diagram that shows the flow of the accounting system using boxes and text to show the logic.

Completing a system flowchart enables improvements to the system, and thus to the company's processes, to be identified.

Activity 2: Flowchart of credit control

Using the pre-seen information on CCC identify the key elements of the accounts receivable process known at this time.

Required

(a) Complete a system flowchart for the accounts receivable function.

(b) Note any gaps in the information which would require further investigation in order to assess the accounting system as it currently stands.

2.1.2 User manuals

Accounting system controls need to be kept under review to ensure they are appropriate and effective, so that the information output from the system is on time and of the correct quality.

> **User manual:** An accurate analysis of how the accounting system and its controls operate, and how they should be used.

To enable this, the accounting function should maintain an accurate user manual of how the accounting system and its controls operate.

Activity 3: Documentation of controls

CCC Ltd is considering developing a full user manual for its accounting system.

Required

(a) What are the advantages of the accounting system having a full user manual for all activities that take place within it?

(b) What might the disadvantages of such an approach be for an organisation like CCC?

3 Sales system controls

The various parts of the accounting system require different internal controls. Here we look at the types of controls that are found in sales systems, and the risks that they are designed to mitigate.

Cash sales are particularly risky, as when a company makes a cash sale no credit is granted. As the customer chooses and pays for goods on the spot, no formal order is raised, resulting in inventory being issued without a sales order form. The risks this poses are discussed later.

In this section, we focus on the correct actions which need to take place to ensure controls are in place. These are the **control objectives** of the credit sales system, and the risks inherent within.

3.1 Controls in the sales system

3.1.1 Segregation of duties

Dividing tasks among several staff members in the sales system, especially in relation to handling cheques and cash receipts, is a key control. By ensuring that one member of staff completes a task, and another reviews the process, it is easier to prevent and detect the following frauds and errors:

(a) **Ghost customers** – creating a false customer who orders goods but does not pay – in effect stealing the company's inventory. This is possible if the same person is in charge of orders and credit control/accounts receivable (receivables ledgers). This risk is mitigated by segregation of duties eg new customers are approved by management, then a different employee enters them onto the system following an external credit check.

(b) **Stolen cash receipts** – cash received is not recorded in the ledgers, it is stolen by employees. Alternatively, an employee could intercept cheques when they arrive and steal them before they are recorded. Segregation of duty is operated here by having the person opening the post supervised during the process.

(c) **Overcharging on sales** – goods sold are overcharged, with employees keeping the additional amount received from customers.

(d) **Inflating customer orders** – additional goods are added to a customer's order, but not invoiced to them. Instead, the excess inventory is retained by the employee for their own use, or to sell on privately.

(e) **Writing off debts** – writing off amounts owed when in fact the debt was paid in full. The employee then keeps the written-off amount.

(f) **Raising credit notes** – that are not sent to the customer, who therefore pays in full. When payment is received in full the employee keeps the cash matching the false credit amount.

(g) **Teeming and lading** – allocating one customer's payment to another in order to balance the books and detract from a shortfall

KEY TERM

> **Authorisation of transactions:** This is a key control activity, indicating to accounting staff that the transaction in question is valid.

Activity 4: Sales controls (1) – customers and orders

The following describes the procedures which CCC currently uses for accepting new customers, taking sales orders and the delivery process.

> While some customers pay cash for their goods, over 60% take credit terms. Customers are granted 28 days to pay their invoice in full, interest free. CCC uses a credit reference agency for orders over £200 to ensure that potential new credit customers have no history of poor payments. Once the agency has done this check, the customer is automatically granted an unlimited line of credit. The sales staff are in charge of calling the credit agency at the time of sale but, as Stefan had recently identified, this does not always happen if junior staff are on duty, or it is a busy day of sales.
>
> All new credit accounts are set up on the first day of the calendar month. All sales orders are received by the showroom store staff for processing, and after completion are passed to the accounting function the next morning, so that Stefan can prepare and record the invoices. Stefan has designed a form in Microsoft Word that he uses as a template for invoicing. All invoices are logged onto an Excel spreadsheet which can be accessed by the accounting team.
>
> The operations manager asks Stefan for a copy of the Excel spreadsheet so he can plan the deliveries for the next week. Once this schedule has been drawn up, the inventory is identified and marked up for delivery. A dispatch note is drawn up and this is handed to the customer. The dispatch note is a manual form which details the customer's address and the invoice reference.
>
> CCC contacts the customers a few days beforehand to agree a delivery time. If the flooring is to be fitted, then the name of the fitter will be supplied. When the flooring has been delivered and fitted, the fitter hands the delivery note to the customer who retains it. The customer does not pay the fitter.

Required

(1) Identify the controls in place at CCC for the sales system; and

(2) Explain the control activities from the control objectives supplied, noting any risks and making any recommendations for improvement.

Control objective	Control activity	Risk and recommendations
Completeness of recording sales		
Record invoices in the correct time period.		
Only creditworthy customers are offered credit terms.		
Record goods dispatched in the inventory system.		

Activity 5: Sales controls (2) – Credit control

The following information has been obtained regarding the cash collection procedures at CCC.

CCC credit control policies

The company policy regarding non-payment is as follows:

- Once payment is seven days overdue Stefan will telephone the customer.

- If payment is not received within 14 days of the telephone call, then Stefan writes to the customer requesting payment and for the account to be brought into order.

- If payment is still not received within the next 14 days, the customer's details are passed on to a debt collection agency which works on behalf of the company. The debt collection agency charges £80 per case, plus 30% of any monies collected.

Though this is the policy, the directors of CCC rarely bother following it through.

As the invoices are manually input onto Word templates, set up by Stefan, he must create an Excel spreadsheet each month to look at what money is owed. He usually rolls forward the spreadsheet from the previous month, but as he is very busy and management do not prompt him, he sometimes misses a month.

Stefan opens the mail every morning and sorts through it. Any cheques received from customers are entered manually into a day book to record the receipt. The day book is then used to update the ledger accounts, and the cheques are placed in the office safe until a banking day.

At the end of every day, all cash and cheques are supposed to be removed from the tills, leaving a float of £100 cash in each till for the start of the next day. The principle is that the till should be balanced to ensure that the cash content is correct.

However, during the week this does not happen as the sales staff feel that they should not be asked to do an extra job after closing. The first salesperson in the next day counts the till contents and takes it upstairs to the accounting office for Stefan to bank it.

As a result, it is common practice that all cash (except for the till floats) and cheques are removed and bagged as takings from individual tills before being stored in the safe in the accounting function office.

Banking

Banking is carried out on Monday and Thursday, and this is normally Stefan's job, which he does during his lunch break.

Recently, available cash from the office safe has been used to pay wages in order to reduce the amount of money drawn from the bank via cheques.

Required

(1) Identify the controls in place at CCC for credit control and cash collection.

(2) Explain the control objectives and activities, noting any risks and making any recommendations for improvement.

Control objective	Control activity	Risk and Recommendations
Record all invoiced sales in the accounting records (receivables ledger and general ledger).		
Record invoiced sales in the correct receivables ledger accounts.		
Identify debts for which payment might be doubtful.		
Record all money received.		

Control objective	Control activity	Risk and Recommendations
Bank all money received.		
Safeguard money received until it is banked.		

4 Purchases system controls

The purchases system – from placing an order to paying the supplier's invoice – is a part of the accounting system which it is particularly important to have controls over because:

(a) The purchases system involves receiving inventory and paying cash – arguably the two types of asset which are most open to fraud and theft.

(b) Purchases may be of very high value, particularly when the company is incurring capital expenditure.

(c) Information from the purchases system becomes part of the data which supports the costing system. Errors and fraud in purchasing will lead to inaccurate information being used for planning, decision making and performance measurement.

(d) The purchase of inventory will affect any manufacturing or retail process. If the information is not accurate, there is a risk of delays to the manufacturing process or delays in fulfilling orders from customers.

4.1 Controls in the purchases system

4.1.1 Segregation of duties

Once again segregation of duties is vital. The chief concern is that a person could order and pay for personal goods through the company, so ordering and payment should be separated.

The risk of fraud will also be reduced if the person who authorises invoices for payments is independent of the person clearing the payment itself.

4.1.2 Authorisation

All purchases should be authorised; however, it would be impractical to have one person authorise every item of expenditure, especially if it required often and in large quantities. To mitigate for this, accounting systems often have set levels of approval for regular purchases, with monitoring controls by management to check over the weekly or monthly expenditure reports. Often there will be maximum amount which will then require management approval, such as £10,000 for a line manager and £50,000 for a director.

Activity 6: Purchases system controls

The following is a summary of the CCC purchases control system:

All inventory is purchased on credit terms from a very wide range of suppliers. This is one of Peter Cookridge's roles, and he enjoys spending time researching new inventory lines. He also likes meeting the sales staff from different suppliers. He has a favourite group of suppliers he tends to use, mainly because they are sometimes willing to sponsor his motorbike and racing efforts. There is no formal list of suppliers.

Margaret Peterson has worked on Excel previously, but this was over ten years ago. While she is competent at inputting data, she sometimes struggles with anything beyond this.

Inventory is ordered by Margaret, who receives the request from the warehouse staff, often verbally, especially if the customer needs the goods urgently. The larger suppliers do provide next-day delivery, which is very useful for CCC.

When the inventory arrives in the warehouse, it is signed for by whomever is available in the warehouse. They should check for any damage, but time is at a premium, and most of the junior staff will accept any delivery and move it to a space in the store. The goods received note (GRN) is put in the in-tray and is taken up to the accounts department when the tray gets full, which is usually once a week.

Margaret will input the invoices she receives (Stefan opens the post and will bring any invoices into the office that same morning) onto the Excel spreadsheet, detailing the following:

- Supplier name
- Description of the item purchased (including dimensions)
- Cost price

If Margaret has a GRN which matches an invoice, she will clip them together and file them away. She uses her Excel spreadsheet as the basis for running the end of month supplier pay run.

Suppliers are paid at the end of the month in which their invoice is received, as long as funds are available. However, some suppliers now request payment within 30 days of the date of invoice, and this is beginning to cause John Cookridge some concern.

CCC holds a large inventory, with many rolls (often older or discontinued ranges) of carpet in the warehouse for sale on a cash basis.

All suppliers are paid by cheque. These are completed by Margaret, and then signed by either John or Peter as they are now the only authorised signatories. The cheque book is stored in a drawer in Margaret's desk in the accounting function office. Occasionally, when the brothers are away from the office for a few days they pre-sign some cheques so that Margaret can make any emergency payments in their absence.

Required

(1) Note FOUR key weaknesses in the CCC purchase and inventory system.

(2) Highlight the risk and propose a suitable control to be implemented by management.

Weakness	Control proposed	Risk controlled

Weakness	Control proposed	Risk controlled

4.2 Non-current assets

Generally, non-current assets purchases are less frequent purchases for an organisation, but the same rules apply in that the expenditure should be authorised.

An organisation will have established rules regarding the purchase of non-current assets, which may look something like this:

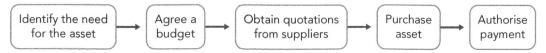

Generally, the budget for a new non-current asset will be approved by a member of the management team, but sometimes, in larger organisations there may be a Budget Committee who will make large, financial decisions. In both cases, a business case together with initial expenditure, estimated payback and useful life will be part of the report submitted for approval.

Increasingly, organisations will want to see what the tax implications would be on such large purchases (eg what are the capital allowances) are there any grants available, maybe the land to be developed is in an area which attracts government funding.

The organisation is likely to have an approved list of suppliers, and several quotations will be obtained to ensure the most suitable price and terms and conditions of purchase.

The payment to be authorised will be agreed against the budgeted figure, and any discrepancies investigated.

5 Payroll system controls

Payroll is a high-risk area, with the segregation of duties and a review of the amounts to be paid mandatory to ensure a robust control environment. Risks are increased if the payroll is run manually and cash is the main basis for payment to staff.

Activity 7: CCC – Payroll controls

The following is some information regarding the payroll system at CCC.

> Until six months ago the payroll was completed by the company's accountants, Bright & Co. Sonja now runs the payroll on a weekly and monthly basis.
>
> The warehouse, delivery and fitting staff are paid weekly in cash. Pay packets are available from the Showroom & Marketing Manager, Jim Andrews, from 10:00 am on a Friday morning.
>
> The rest of the staff are paid monthly, by BACS, on the last working day of each month.
>
> Sales staff earn a commission of 2% on the first £7,500 of sales per month, and 5% on any sales over that figure. John Cookridge is responsible for preparing los to ensure that there is adequate staff coverage for all opening hours. Most of the sales staff are willing to work overtime, so this does not usually create any problems.
>
> Fitters are assigned to their respective duties on a weekly basis and are usually notified on a Monday morning when they arrive at work.
>
> Once the week has finished, the completed rotas are given to Sonja, who uses them to calculate the amount of hours that the individual employees have worked.
>
> Sonja prepares the payslips from this information on a Wednesday, calculating manually any overtime payments due and any Sunday working. From this, she calculates how much cash needs to be drawn from the bank and uses the company cheque book (which is kept locked in Margaret's desk) to prepare a cheque ready for signing.
>
> On a Thursday she prepares the pay packets, which are stored in the office safe for Jim to collect and hand out to the staff the following day, though any member of sales staff who is not busy will actually do this. Any pay packets not given out are returned to the office safe by Sonja and remain there until collected by the relevant member of staff.
>
> Salaried staff are paid monthly on the last working day of the month, and this is done using BACS. The BACS information is prepared by Sonja, signed by either of the directors, and needs to be with the bank by the 25th of each month. The directors will check the salaried staff payments to Sonja's calculation schedule. Sonja can input the details onto the bank system for the payments and can authorise the payments up to a value of £10,000 per BACS run. This is adequate to cover the salaried staff, except if the commissions are high or at Christmas. Then the BACS run must be further authorised on the banking software by one of the authorised signatories. No further checks are made by the directors.
>
> Envelopes with payslips are handed to each member of the salaried staff by Sonja on the day they are paid. If a staff member is not available, the envelope is placed in their desk drawer.
>
> There is no requirement, or system in place, for either store or office employees to sign in or out when they start or finish work.

Required

(1)   Document the payroll controls currently in place at CCC.

(2)   Consider where any control weaknesses lie, and what control activities should be introduced to mitigate risks to the company.

Payroll control in place	Control weakness	Suggested control to be introduced

Payroll control in place	Control weakness	Suggested control to be introduced

Assessment focus point

The activities in this chapter are to enable you to practise identifying the key risks, weaknesses and controls in place in different systems. In the exam, you may be asked specific questions regarding controls over trade receivables (consider the sales cycle), inventory and work in progress (think about purchases controls). Consider also the differences between service, manufacturing and retail industries.

6 The risk assessment process

Risk assessment process: This includes the following: identify the risk; evaluate the risk; respond to the risk (manage/mitigate risk by taking appropriate action); ensure compliance (legal and regulatory); monitor, review and report.

As discussed earlier, management should regularly review the controls that are in place. Any review should include an assessment of any new risks, internal (such as a new computer system or management restructure) and external (increased market competition, issues with suppliers etc) that may impact the organisation. In doing so, any review should assess the ability of the internal control system to respond to the risk that:

(a) Objectives might not be met – including the company's sustainability and corporate social reporting (CSR) objectives (eg sales targets, waste disposal, staff training requirements and recruitment concerns)

(b) The company may be the victim of loss or fraud – can be accidental or intended, and arise from internal or external sources

(c) The system may contain errors that result in misstatement in the financial statements – eg assets overvalued and/or liabilities understated

(d) The company is engaged in unethical behaviour – either intentionally (eg due to pressures to achieve unrealistic sales targets) or unintentionally (eg poorly trained staff taking on new tasks)

(e) The company fails to comply with its legal obligations – such as non-compliance with company law or health and safety regulations

The risk assessment process must be robust to reduce or avoid these risks. The main aim of analysing the risk of fraud is assessing the likelihood on the fraud occurring and its impact if it does occur and seeking out ways to minimise the risk.

KEY TERM

> **Risk of fraud:** The likelihood of the fraud occurring and its impact if it does occur.

Activity 8: Payroll risks

The following is some additional information on CCC regarding an event during October 20X2. You may also wish to refer to the payroll information given in Activity 7.

> Sonja, the payroll clerk, was approached once again by Ron Sellers, one of the sales team. He had been expecting commission totalling £1,200 in his wages for October but complained to Sonja that this had not correctly calculated and subsequently he had been underpaid. Ron was cross and aggressively told Sonja that he really needed the missing money right now.
>
> Sonja was so upset by this that she told Ron that she would borrow the money out of the petty cash tin and replace it when she made his wages up. Ron calmed down and said he would collect it from her at the end of the day and stated that he hoped it 'wouldn't happen again'.
>
> Joe Bloggins spoke to Sonja and explained that he had taken on an extra member of staff for the Christmas rush and January sales. Joe said that the new employee would be paid on an hourly basis, and that as he was a student, he would not pay tax, and could be paid weekly – in cash. Sonja asked for the new starter document that all new employees had to complete, but Joe insisted this was not necessary for temporary staff, and insisted Sonja just add him to the payroll system. Joe said that he would send through the completed document later in the week. Sonja agreed, and added the new worker, Andrew Lias, to the payroll, leaving herself a diary note to ask Joe for the documentation the next week if it was still outstanding.
>
> Sonja's day was made even worse by the printer jamming, resulting in several of the payslips being printed upside down. Sonja was so fed up, she screwed the partially torn and smudged payslips into a ball and threw them in the bin, assured the directors that she would re-run the payslips first thing the next day, and went home early.

 BPP

Required

Prepare a risk assessment summary for the payroll system for the directors of CCC. Highlight the key issues which have occurred in the payroll system during October and what regulatory and ethical risks these pose to the organisation.

To: The Directors of CCC
Risk assessment of the payroll system based on events in October 20X2

7 Fraud matrix

> **Fraud matrix:** A map of the potential frauds against an organisation, cross-referenced to the risks of each of these occurring, documenting the controls over these risks. Also known as a risk matrix.

A fraud matrix helps the company:

- Investigate the **potential** for fraud within a system
- Analyse the **controls** currently in place to prevent fraud
- **Grade the potential** for fraud, according to risk

Although this approach is subjective, it enables a risk-based approach to improving controls that are appropriate to the company.

The risk to the company is graded on an appropriate scale, either numerically on a scale of 1–5 or by stating the deemed level of risk.

- 1 = low
- 3 = medium
- 5 = high

Possible improvements to the controls for all high and/or medium risks can then be recommended.

7.1 Identifying the grade of risk

The level of risk of fraud in a particular situation is graded as high, medium or low by identifying two factors:

- The **likelihood** of the risk occurring; and
- The potential **impact** of that risk on the company.

Illustration 1: CCC

In looking at the potential for the misappropriation of petty cash in CCC:

- The likelihood is high (5): loose cash is easy to steal and it presents a strong temptation, especially in small amounts, as the person stealing it may not perceive the loss to be that 'bad' a thing for the company.
- The impact on the company is medium (3), as the company could potentially lose £1,200.

Combining these two factors, the overall risk of fraud in relation to petty cash would probably be graded as medium/high (4).

Activity 9: Fraud matrix CCC

Using your knowledge obtained to date of CCC, answer the following questions. (Use the table given to guide your answer).

Required

Complete the fraud matrix below in respect of CCC. In particular you should:

(1)   Identify FOUR risks to CCC which may not be prevented or detected by the existing controls currently in place.

(2)   Identify any regulation or law which could be broken by CCC as a result of these risks and the possible impact on the organisation.

	Potential fraud	Controls currently in place	Risk to CCC 1 = low 5 = high	Implications/ Regulations affected
1				
2				

Potential fraud	Controls currently in place	Risk to CCC 1 = low 5 = high	Implications/ Regulations affected
3			
4			

8 Monitoring controls

Controls must be monitored to assess their effectiveness over time.

This review is usually overseen by management or, in larger organisations, an independent internal audit team. Internal auditors will review controls across different departments within the company. The role of internal audit differs from that of the external audit. The external auditors review the year-end financial statements and give an opinion as to whether the statements represent a true and fair view of the company. Occasionally, both sets of auditors will work alongside each other, such as when the external auditors are assessing the controls within an IT system. However, it is important to note that whilst internal auditors are employed by the organisation, the external auditors are not. External auditors are typically engaged to assess the financial records on behalf of a company's shareholders for legal compliance purposes.

In smaller organisations, effective monitoring can take place, formally or informally, by function heads. For example, the sales director is likely to become aware of control deficiencies in the sales cycle, as they are responsible for managing the sales department's ongoing performance, so will investigate any reasons behind poor performance.

Assessment focus point

For the INAC assessment, you are expected to be able to propose **monitoring**, **review** and **report** actions in response to an identified risk. It is important that you can define these terms in order to be able to apply them to a scenario.

KEY TERM

Monitoring, review and report: In this context, **monitoring** means looking at activity or behaviour related to a specified fraud risk because you need to know the extent of this activity or behaviour.

Review means gathering evidence of this activity or behaviour to understand the extent of this fraud risk.

Report means what you communicate to those higher up in the organisation as part of the overall risk management process.

Illustration 2: Monitoring, review and report at CCC

The fraud matrix that was completed for CCC included a number of fraud risks. For example:

- Overstatement of wages - additional cash being paid to staff for work not done
- Theft of inventory from the warehouse
- Writing off customer debts without authorisation

Required

How would you monitor, review and report on these fraud risks?

Fraud risk	Monitoring (activity/behaviour)	Review (evidence to collect)	Report (what gets communicated)
Overstatement of wages - additional cash being paid to staff for work not done			
Theft of inventory from the warehouse			
Writing off customer debts without authorisation			

Solution

Fraud risk	Monitoring (activity/behaviour)	Review (evidence to collect)	Report (what gets communicated)
Overstatement of wages - additional cash being paid to staff for work not done	Budget overspend or adverse variance. Payments outside of contracted terms	Comparison of contract rates with actual payments. Reconciliation of wage rates to employees' contracts of employment	Amount of any wage overspend by cause (not due to overtime or prior period error)
Theft of inventory from the warehouse	Inventory recorded as received but unable to be found when required	Instances of inventory leaving the warehouse without a legitimate reason (eg valid sales order)	Amount of inventory moved without legitimate documentation
Writing off customer debts without authorisation	Sales that are cancelled by staff without the appropriate authority	Sales written off without appropriate supporting documentation (eg credit note or journal approved by a senior member of staff)	Percentage of sales written off without appropriate supporting documentation

 BPP

Chapter summary

- The accounting system processes raw data on transactions into outputs to meet the information needs of stakeholders.
- An effective accounting system operates effectively, reports accurately, and complies with applicable laws and regulations.
- Controls in an accounting system allow it to effectively and accurately meet internal and external regulations, and the information needs of stakeholders.
- A user manual documents the accounting system and enables its effectiveness to be kept under review.
- Threats to the accounting system's security include human error, data loss, malicious damage and fraud.
- Security controls include controls over the integrity of data and processing, the system itself, and physical access to the system.
- Using and updating strong passwords are key security controls.
- Flowcharting the accounting system and internal controls enables a systems analyst to see whether controls have been designed effectively.
- The fundamental principles of professional ethics are: integrity; objectivity; professional competence and due care; confidentiality; and professional behaviour.
- The accounting system needs to be operated in an ethical manner, following the five fundamental principles, in order to meet its objectives.
- Fraud is a crime in which the company suffers a loss because someone either misappropriates assets or misstates information in the financial statements.
- Misappropriation can take the form of: theft of assets; teeming and lading of receipts (receivables ledger) and payments (payables ledger); setting up fictitious suppliers, employees or customers; collusion with customers and suppliers; paying for goods and services not received by the company; and disposal of assets without authority.
- Misstatement of the financial statements arises from: over- or undervaluing inventory; not writing off irrecoverable debts; manipulating accounting estimates to affect profit; fictitious sales; and understating expenses.
- Prevention controls for fraud comprise: authorisation; segregation of duties; and review procedures.
- Fraud controls for the accounting system are categorised as staff, management, physical and computer controls.
- A fraud matrix (or risk matrix) maps potential frauds to the risk to the company and controls over that risk.
- The risk of fraud is graded from low (1) to high (5) on the fraud matrix; more attention is devoted to internal controls over the higher risks.
- Detection controls over fraud comprise: spot checks; performance reviews; reconciliation procedures; and control accounts.
- Ratio analysis is a key way in which statutory financial statements are analysed by both internal and external stakeholders.
- Sales system frauds are typically: stealing cash receipts; overcharging for sales; inflating customer orders; writing off debts; raising credit notes; and teeming and lading.
- Purchases system frauds include: ordering goods for own use; paying fictitious suppliers; paying funds into personal bank accounts; and teeming and lading.
- Payroll system frauds may involve: ghost employees; overstating overtime pay; unauthorised increases in pay rates; false expense reimbursements; and retained leavers.
- Fraud affects the company in terms of: financial loss; reputational damage; and poor employee morale.

 BPP

Activity answers

Activity 1: CCC accounting system

(a) The current IT system is Microsoft Office based and CCC does not use a bespoke or 'off the shelf' accounting system such as Sage or a cloud accounting system such as Xero. There are therefore no annual or monthly fees, making this a very cheap system to maintain.

However, most of the activities that the staff are required to do, such as raising invoices and preparing summary reports, take longer to complete because they use a Word template and this requires manual calculations.

Due to the manual nature of most of the transactions completed by staff, this can make the accounting system overly time consuming to update and use, as well as more open to human error.

(b) Information is produced by the team when requested by management, apart from the quarterly reports set as standard (summary of financial revenue and expenses and a budgetary control report).

Although management have not yet noticed any issues regarding reliability of the IT system, the computers used by the staff are all 'stand alone' and do not network. Therefore, the computers do not 'talk' to each other, and information may be missed or even duplicated. Currently, only one member of staff actively backs up their data. There is a high risk that data may be lost if the computers crash. There is a risk that the information produced may be inconsistent with reporting requirements, eg accuracy of the VAT and PAYE reporting due to the manual calculations involved.

(c) Given the manual element of the system, it takes longer and is more labour intensive to prepare internal reports, such as management accounts. The management accounts are only prepared quarterly for this reason, and it can take up to 20 days for them to be completed. Whilst this seems slow it may be entirely acceptable to the directors of CCC.

Overall: Although the current IT system costs little to maintain, it is not cost effective in terms of usage due to the manual nature of the processes undertaken by staff. This causes information output delays, and there is also a risk of data loss.

Activity 2: Flowchart of credit control

(a)

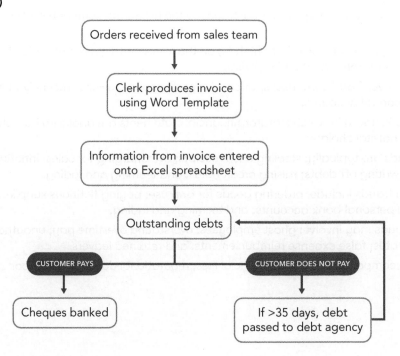

(b) Information which needs to be investigated further to ensure the flowchart is complete and to fully assess the accounting system for credit control:

- How are the debts chased by the team; are the customers phoned or letters written? Who is responsible for this role?

- Does management ever review the aged receivables report to decide whether any debts need to be classified as irrecoverable?

- What happens if the debt collection agency is unsuccessful?

- Can customers pay directly via BACS? How are these receipts identified and allocated to customers' accounts?

Activity 3: Documentation of controls

(a) Fraud matrix

Advantages of a user manual for CCC's accounting system:

- Quick and efficient training of new staff

- Better visibility of the controls in place

- Consistent approach to completing activities

- Easier to rotate staff between roles and responsibilities

- Easier to evaluate staff against standard procedures

- Improved supervisory and management control

(b) Disadvantages of a user manual:

- Increased risk of 'outsiders' being able to operate the system especially as the door to the accounting function is usually left open and the office unsecured.

- Procedures may stifle innovation and improvements to processes.

- User manuals take time to complete, and the accounting function at CCC is very short on resources currently, so this may take up too much time to the detriment of the day to day business.

- The manuals may become out of date quickly and a small company like CCC may not have time to regularly review and update the manuals.

- The manuals need to be tested to ensure they accurately reflect the systems in place.

- Staff often do not conform to manuals, negating the benefits of having them.

 BPP

Activity 4: Sales controls (1) – customers and orders

Control objective	Control activity	Risk and recommendations
Completeness of recording sales	Sales orders are manually entered onto the system.	No pre-ordered invoice numbering, which allows for orders to be missed (customers taking goods without being invoiced). Manual system, open to error as the invoices are manually calculated on a Word template. Customer may be incorrectly invoiced, which could lead to loss of revenue or reputation if a customer is charged in error. Recommendation: To buy an integrated accounting system with orders matching to invoices which are system calculated with pre-numbered invoices to ensure completeness.
Record invoices in the correct time period.	Implement cut-off procedures (eg at each month-end review) to ensure outstanding orders are recorded in the correct month.	Invoices for new customers are not set up until the next month, so invoices are not recorded in the correct period. New customers should be set up prior to sales being authorised.
Only creditworthy customers are offered credit terms.	Credit checks on all orders over £200 to be completed at the point of sale.	Risk that CCC may incur financial losses due to not all customers being credit checked. Staff should be trained on how the checks are completed. Manager authorisation of initial credit sales to new customers should be established to ensure that all sales with credit terms have been adequately checked. The unlimited credit line should be replaced with hard limits that can only be increased with the authority of the directors once a track record of reliable payment has been established.

BPP

Control objective	Control activity	Risk and recommendations
Record goods dispatched in the inventory system.	Inventory marked up for delivery and a dispatch note manually raised	Dispatch of goods should be authorised by appropriate personnel and agreed back to order documents. Dispatched goods should be inspected for quality and quantity. Dispatch notes should be sequentially numbered and the sequence should be checked regularly. Inventory records should be updated from goods sent out records. Unfulfilled orders should be regularly reviewed.

Activity 5: Sales controls (2) – Credit control

Control objective	Control activity	Risk and Recommendations
Record all invoiced sales in the accounting records (receivables ledger and general ledger).	Sales invoice sequence should be recorded and spoilt invoices recorded and destroyed.	Sales not recorded and wrongly omitted from financial statements. Payment not chased as the sale was never recorded. Perform regular reconciliations between sales invoices and receivables ledgers.
Record invoiced sales in the correct receivables ledger accounts.	Receivables statements should be prepared and checked regularly; this is especially important with CCC as it has a manual system where invoices are input onto a spreadsheet, so the margin for error is greater. Receivables statements should be safeguarded so they cannot be amended before they are sent out (password protected). Accounts receivable control account should be reconciled regularly to the receivables ledger.	Loss of custom by chasing the wrong customer for the debt. Not receiving the money from the correct customer. If the invoice is not entered onto the sales Excel spreadsheet then the debt may not get chased at all. This is one of the reasons CCC should consider a more integrated system.

Control objective	Control activity	Risk and Recommendations
Identify debts for which payment might be doubtful.	Overdue accounts should be reviewed and followed up. Regular review of the aged receivables report by staff and by management. Write-off of irrecoverable debts should be authorised by appropriate personnel.	Failure to take action until it is too late to recover the debt. Irrecoverable debts misstated as assets in the financial statements. Currently CCC has no regular review process for the aged receivables and no formalised method of reviewing the write-off of irrecoverable debts. Risk that valid and recoverable debts may be incorrectly written off.
Record all money received.	Supervise opening the post to avoid interception. There should be appropriate arrangements made when cashiers are on holiday. Receipts books should be serially numbered and kept locked up. Sales receipts should be matched with invoices. Customer remittance advices should be retained.	Money could be stolen or lost. Custom lost through chasing payments already made by the customer. Financial statements misstated. Risk that only one person opening the post and also recording any payments received may contribute to fraud or loss of cash or cheques (intentional or otherwise). Customers should be encouraged to pay via online banking or using cards in the shop.
Bank all money received.	Till rolls should be reconciled to cash collections which should then be agreed to cash banked. Cash and cheques should be banked daily. Paying in books should be compared to initial cash records. All receipts should be banked together. Where cards are taken in the shop, the card reader end-of-day report should reconcile to the card payments received in the till.	Money could be stolen or lost as banking is currently only completed twice a week. Custom lost through chasing payments already made by the customer Financial statements misstated. Company cannot earn interest on money if it is not banked, or pays additional overdraft interest.

Control objective	Control activity	Risk and Recommendations
Safeguard money received until it is banked.	There should be restrictions on who is allowed to accept cash (cashiers or salespeople). Cash received should be evidenced (till rolls, receipts). Cash registers should be regularly emptied. Cash shortages should be investigated. Opening of new bank accounts should be restricted to certain personnel and authorised by senior management. Cash floats held should be limited. Restrictions should be in place when making payments from cash received. Restrictions should be in place for access to cash on the premises. Cash floats should be checked by an independent person, sometimes on a surprise basis. Cash should be locked up outside normal business hours.	Money may be stolen in the interim period. Differences between the sales recorded in the tills and the cash actually received may go unnoticed and errors occur in the financial records. Banking should be more regular, and the company should consider only accepting payment via card to avoid cash-based risks altogether.

Activity 6: Purchases system controls

Any four from the examples listed below.

Weakness	Control proposed	Risk controlled
Goods and services can be ordered for any purpose – personal or the company's benefit.	Necessity for orders should be evidenced before orders are authorised. Only prepare orders when purchase requisitions are received from relevant departments. Pre-number and safeguard blank order forms. Orders not yet received should be reviewed.	Company pays for unnecessary or personal goods.
Any suppliers can be used – no approved list.	Have a central policy for choosing suppliers. Monitor supplier terms and take advantage of discounts offered.	Unauthorised suppliers may not supply quality goods or may be too expensive. New suppliers may not offer credit terms, so cash flow is affected as the supplier must be paid prior to delivery.

Weakness	Control proposed	Risk controlled
No checks prior to inputting the invoice onto the Excel spreadsheet are completed back to the original order or the GRN.	Check invoices to purchase orders and GRNs to verify what was received.	Risk that invoices may not match what was ordered or what was received. Check invoices for prices, quantities and calculations.
Invoices are not logged when they arrive at CCC.	Reference invoices (stamp with sequential number and supplier reference). This will ensure that **all** invoices received go through the review and payment process.	Risk that invoices get missed when they arrive in the post. Company fails to pay for goods/services and loses suppliers.
Currently, CCC only pays invoices at the end of the month.	The spreadsheet should detail the terms and conditions for the invoice, and any payment terms and whether any settlement or early discount can be taken. This would be significantly easier and be an automatic procedure if CCC had accounting software instead of a manual system.	Company may miss early settlement discounts or promotions, thus paying more for inventory.
There is no mention of how CCC can prevent paying a supplier twice. The spreadsheet does not appear to be updated once the payment has been made and there is a risk that cheques could be delayed in the post and a new one written if the supplier chases for payment.	Payments should be recorded promptly in the cash book and ledger. Propose that BACS payments (which are easily traceable and quicker) are used instead of cheques.	Company pays more than once and the supplier does not correct the mistake.
Goods are only checked for damage when they arrive; they are not verified to any order number.	Verify all incoming inventory back to a purchase order or purchase order listing (this may be manual in the case of CCC). Confirm that the inventory has been received and ensure the GRN is promptly sent to the accounts office (stamping the GRN with a sequential number so that the accounting team can see whether any GRNs are missing).	There is a risk that unordered, incorrect or wrong goods are accepted upon delivery.

Weakness	Control proposed	Risk controlled
Cheques are the only method provided for CCC paying its suppliers. This can delay payment if the signatory is not available leading to the use of pre-signed cheques.	Cheques should be requisitioned and requests evidenced with supporting documentation. Cheque payments should be authorised by someone other than a signatory. Cheques should never be signed before the amount and the payee are completed. Signed cheques should be dispatched promptly.	Only make payments to the correct recipients and for the correct amounts which are authorised.
Purchase orders are not ticked off by the accounting team, so they are not aware of what invoices they are expecting. Equally, GRNs are not verified and checked against invoices received on a systematic basis. There is a risk that goods may have arrived but not be invoiced (accrual at year end missing) or an invoice has been received but no goods (in which case, the invoice should not be paid until receipt).	Purchase order listing should be regularly reviewed and any missing orders chased up. GRNs should be matched to orders and invoices matched to GRNs. GRNs should be verified and checked against invoices received on a systematic basis.	Financial statements may be misstated by recording a purchase but not inventory, or recording inventory but not the associated liability. Penalty from HMRC for recording VAT in the wrong VAT period.

Activity 7: CCC – Payroll controls

Payroll control in place	Control weakness	Suggested control to be introduced
Cash is kept in the petty cash tin and locked in the safe at night. Cash wages are kept in the safe once calculated. They are handed to Jim, Showroom & the Marketing Manager for distribution (see weakness).	The use of cash to pay wages could lead to the payroll staff colluding with weekly staff and adding more cash to the pay packet than the amount earned or shown on the wages slip. Although wages should be handed out by Jim, this can be overridden if he is busy.	BACS payments to be introduced for all staff to ensure only fully validated amounts are received by staff (and fully traceable if there is a dispute). Cash wages should cease. Payslips could be posted to the home address. If cash wages retained: Identity of staff should be verified before payment (with wages being signed out by staff). Distributions of cash wages should be recorded.
Staff rotas with details of hours worked are sent by the managers to the payroll clerk.	Gross pay is calculated manually, which increases the risk of errors. There is no verification of when staff start or finish, as no time records are kept.	Introduce a payroll system which calculates gross pay based on hours worked instead of manual calculation. Regular checks should be carried out of the payroll records against the HR records and vice versa. If retaining manual system, ensure that another member of staff verifies the calculation.
Payroll clerk counts out the cash and draws up the BACS listing.	Errors can occur or additional amounts be added to the cash wages.	Segregation of duty of the calculation and payment of wages and salaries. BACS payments should be verified by management once set up on the system by the payroll clerk; however, they only agree to the calculation (the calculation is not verified). Bank transfer lists should be prepared and authorised. Bank transfer lists should be compared to the payroll.

Payroll control in place	Control weakness	Suggested control to be introduced
Deductions are calculated by payroll clerk using tax tables (see pre-seen scenario).	Errors can occur and incorrect deductions possibly made. Risk that incorrect submissions are made to HMRC.	Ensure all deductions have been properly calculated and authorised. Consider outsourcing to a payroll bureau, or using approved HMRC software to comply with RTI requirements.

Activity 8: Payroll risks

To: The Directors of CCC
Risk assessment of the payroll system based on events in October 20X2
There is a high risk of errors in the payroll system due to:

- Unauthorised additional payments to staff taking place
- Sales commission not being checked by a member of management (for example, the sales manager) prior to payment.
- New starters being put onto the system without any documentation or checks documented regarding their hours, contract and terms and conditions, or whether they actually exist.
- Large amounts of cash kept on the premises with staff being able to top up wages by taking £1,200 out of petty cash without any safeguards, checks or authorisation in place.
- There being no controls over the hours and rates that staff are being paid. There is a risk that these could be amended resulting in staff being paid too much.

Risk of regulatory failure due to:

- New starters being paid on the system prior to the tax information being received. There is a risk that their deductions will be incorrect, risking penalties from HMRC or complaints from staff affected.
- Spoilt payslips being thrown away and not correctly destroyed. This is a confidentiality risk and puts the company at risk of breach of data protection regulations.
- The payroll clerk has had no further training since she qualified four years ago. There is no mention of what qualification she currently has or any required continuing professional development. It is possible that new regulations are missed and the company may be fined (eg there is no pension scheme despite this being a legal requirement for all employers in the UK).
- No checks on proof of identity are made, or references required when new staff members join. This could expose the company to risk of theft as well as breaches of money laundering regulations.

Risk of ethical breaches occurring in the workplace due to:

- Bullying and intimidation of payroll staff by members of the sales team – see Ron's treatment of Sonja. All staff should be treated with respect; aggressive and threatening behaviour should not be tolerated.
- Breach of confidentiality by leaving spoilt payslips with employee information in the bin rather than being destroyed.

Activity 9: Fraud matrix CCC

This fraud matrix suggests improvements to the controls CCC currently has in place. They have to be appropriate to the company; we could not suggest, for instance, full segregation of duties within CCC as there are not enough staff working within the accounting function to make this possible. Also, the assessment of risk is subjective based on our knowledge of the company and the controls currently in place.

Potential fraud	Controls currently in place	Risk to CCC 1 = low, 5 = high	Implications/ Regulations affected
Theft of assets	Physical access to the accounting function controlled by keypad but with common entry code, and door left propped open.	2	Loss of assets such as computers and possibly key data and information Financial loss
Overstatement of wages – Wages Clerk Additional monies being paid to staff without the formal support of payroll records	None	4	Overpayment of wages to staff Financial loss
Theft of cash from the office	Petty cash is kept in the staff room and office has keypad access, but is left propped open. Contains notebook for recording expenses charged to petty cash, but this control is often not followed.	3	Loss of cash
Theft of cheques	Cheque book kept in locked drawer – but control not always followed.	4	Cheques could be used for own purchase/cash Financial loss
Overstatement of hours worked – showroom supervisor	None	3	Overpayment of wages to showroom staff
Theft of inventory from warehouse	An Excel spreadsheet showing inventory levels and location of inventory is in place; however, this document is not always updated and inventory checks back to it do not tend to occur.	4	Loss of inventory
Fictitious suppliers could be entered onto the system and payments made	None	4	Financial loss

Potential fraud	Controls currently in place	Risk to CCC 1 = low, 5 = high	Implications/ Regulations affected
Overpayment of supplier invoices	None	3	Increased costs Financial loss
Under-recording of goods sold	None	3	Reduced revenue
Writing off customer debts without authorisation	None	3	Financial loss risk due to monies which are recovered being misappropriated whilst the debt is wrongly written off Reputational risk as customer will be unhappy by the chasing of an already paid debt
Theft of cheques from the mail	Cheques received are written into day book by the same person who opens the post. There is no segregation of duty here; it would be better for Stefan to wait until another member of staff is present to witness the opening of post.	2	Lost cheques, reduced revenue Reputational risk as customer will be unhappy by the chasing of an already paid debt
Theft of cash/cheques from the tills	None – tills are not reconciled until the following day.	3	Lost cash/cheques
Theft of wages arising from the payment to a ghost employee	Documentary evidence should be provided before any new starter can be set up on the payroll system; however, there is evidence that this is not always the case.	3	Lost cash/increased costs
Disclosure of staff information without the proper authority	None	3	Potential fine or penalties caused by breach of the data protection Regulations

Potential fraud	Controls currently in place	Risk to CCC 1 = low, 5 = high	Implications/ Regulations affected
Peter Cookridge buying inventory higher than usual to benefit personally from the supplier who will support his motorcycling	None	4	Cash flow issues Too high an inventory level (affecting working capital) Financial loss Potential breach of the Bribery Act 2010

Test your learning

1 Identify the type of control being demonstrated in the activities below. Select the option from the picklist; some of the options may be used more than once or not at all.

Activities	Type of security control
Batch processing of invoices	▼
Only the finance manager can authorise new suppliers on the system	▼
Sequential numbering of invoices	▼
Alerts to the user when the journal being entered does not balance	▼

Picklist

- Completeness
- Integrity
- Processing
- Segregation of duties

2 An accounting system should meet the expectations and requirements of the organisation.

Required

Select the key objectives of the accounting system from the selection below.

Tick ALL that apply.

	✓
Cost effectiveness	
Ease of use	
Reliable	
Providing timely information	

3 Complete the following statement.

The requirement for an accountant to act diligently is part of the fundamental principle of

 .

Picklist

- Integrity
- Objectivity
- Professional behaviour
- Professional competence and due care

4 Which TWO factors are evaluated to grade the risk of fraud in a fraud matrix?

	✓
Time	
Responsibility	
Likelihood	
Volatility	
Impact	

5 The THREE categories of impact of fraud on a company are:

	✓
Morale	
Social	
Reputation	
Environmental	
Financial	

6 Which of the following statements is correct?

	✓
During the analysis of the sales system, a fraud matrix graded the potential loss from misappropriation to be rated 5. Management have decided urgent action is required.	
A fraud matrix is a subjective analysis of an organisation's controls, and will ensure that all recommendations identified are actioned immediately.	
A control within the payroll system has been rated as 2 within the fraud matrix. Management have decided that this risk must be rectified immediately.	

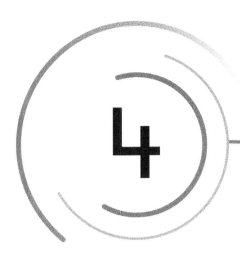

Impact of technology

Learning outcomes

4.1 Reporting information using technology

Learners need to understand:

4.1.1 how accounting software presents data to non-financial managers

4.1.2 how visualisation improves financial understanding of managers and clients

4.2 Using technology within the accounting system

Learners need to understand:

4.2.1 how technological changes may affect the accounting systems:

- cloud accounting:
  - remote access
  - share access
  - improved sustainability
  - control of data
  - reliance on access to technology
- artificial intelligence (AI) and machine learning:
  - change in staffing levels
  - change in error rates
  - implementation and running costs
- data analytics:
  - speeds up processes and decision making
  - may reduce risk of fraud
  - identifying opportunities in a business to work smarter, focus and prioritise

4.2.2 that there are different types of data analytics:

- descriptive
- diagnostic
- predictive
- prescriptive

4.2.3 the requirement for data security

4.2.4 the risks to data and operation caused by:

- cyberattacks (phishing, malware, denial of service)
- unauthorised access (remote or physical)
- physical loss of equipment
- data issued in error.

Assessment context

The topics covered in this chapter will be included within a number of tasks in the Internal Accounting Systems and Controls unit assessment.

Qualification context

This unit builds on the information introduced in the Level 3 *Business Awareness* unit.

Business context

The use of technology in accounting is growing rapidly and it is import that you understand the impact that these changes have on accounting procedures. For example, cloud accounting has revolutionised the way in which small businesses keep their accounts: data has become more detailed, more focused and presented in various visual ways that make it easier to understand.

Data security and breaches are regularly reported in the press, and therefore it is imperative that you understand the importance of keeping all data secure and consider the confidential nature of the data that you will be processing as part of your everyday role.

Chapter overview

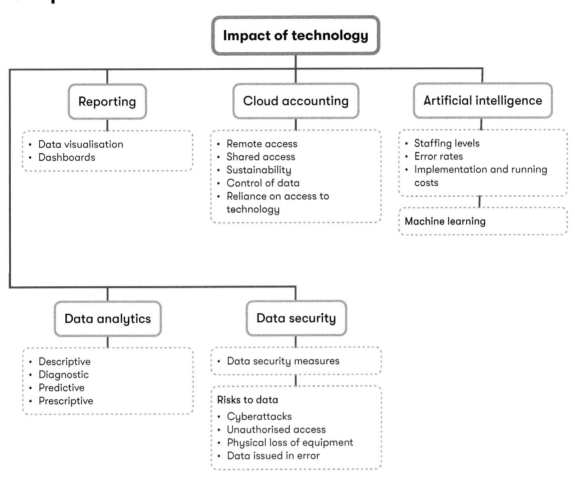

Introduction

In this chapter, we will look at the ways in which technology can enhance the reporting of financial information both internally within a business and to external stakeholders.

New technologies such as cloud accounting, artificial intelligence (AI) and data analytics have all had an impact on the accounting systems used by business which will be explored.

With the ever-increasing use of technology, data security is an area of risk which must be addressed as any breaches might be critical to a business and/or breach laws or regulations.

1 Reporting financial information using technology

There have been significant advances in the way in which financial information can now be presented using accounting software. Historically, the reports generated by accounting software usually contained tables of figures which often then had to be explained or interpreted by accountants for other users to be able to understand the data. Information sometimes had to be manually collated using spreadsheets or other programs to bring together data from different systems.

Data can now be quickly presented in a number of ways which make it more accessible for users.

1.1 Data visualisation

> **Data visualisation:** The representation of information in the form of a graph, picture, chart etc which will allow the user to see the patterns and outliers in a data set.

A data visualisation is usually created at a certain moment, or period, or time. Data visualisation tools and technologies can be useful for analysing massive amounts of information and making data-driven decisions.

They are also a key tool in making financial information more understandable and accessible to non-accountants, both internally within a company and also for external stakeholders. A well designed chart or graph makes it easier to identify patters and trends and understand the key features of the data being presented.

Some common data visualisations are bar charts, line graphs, dashboards, tables, mapping charts and pie charts.

Many annual reports now make use of data visualisations. For example, the BAE Systems 2020 annual report has the following visualisation to show the geographical spread of employees.

Employees by location

BAE Systems employs a skilled workforce of 89,600 people[2] in more than 40 countries.

A	UK	35,300
B	US	31,900
C	Saudi Arabia	6,700
D	Australia	4,500
E	Other	11,200
Total employees[2]		89,600

Internal department and board reports can also make use of data visualisations to present financial and non-financial information clearly to non-accountants.

Activity 1: Data visualisation

Choose the appropriate term from the picklist below to show the method of data visualisation being described:

	Picklist
This data visualisation method provides a summary of four or five relevant drivers that give an overview of a business area.	▼
This data visualisation method is often used to show trend analysis.	▼

Picklist

- Bar charts
- Dashboards
- Line charts
- Mapping charts
- Pie charts
- Tables

1.2 Dashboards

KEY TERM

Dashboard reporting: A visual representation of a company's key performance indicators (KPIs) using data visualisations.

Dashboard: Uses real time data from the company's accounting and other systems to give an accessible overview of the company's performance.

Key performance indicator: The metric or information needed by management to assess the performance of a part, or all, of the business.

Dashboards make use of data visualisations but use real time data. For example, a dashboard could be created for the sales team showing the sales made in each location daily.

Dashboards can bring together information from the accounting software system as well as other data sources like customer information.

The information represented in a dashboard should be the indicators that management use to measure the performance of that part of the business, sometimes referred to as key performance indicators. It is important to involve the users of the dashboard in its design to ensure that it contains the information that they need to see in a user-friendly and accessible way. The data should be clearly presented without unnecessary distractions.

An illustrative data dashboard for cash management has been created by the software developer, Datapine.

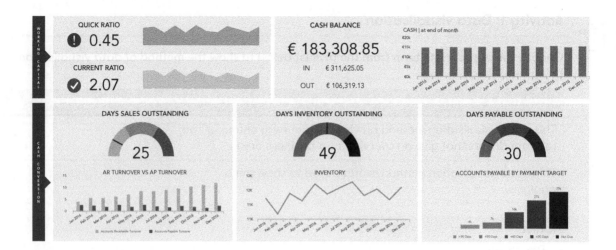

2 Cloud accounting

The concept of cloud accounting was introduced in the Level 3 unit *Business Awareness.*

Cloud accounting: Allows users to remotely access the accountancy software from any location or computer.

2.1 Impact of cloud accounting

Traditionally, accounting software had to be installed on a server or individual computer. This has the benefit of staff being able to work from anywhere which provides **flexibility** and accessibility to financial and other data held on the cloud.

In addition, **multiple users** can gain access to the data **simultaneously** rather than only one user being able to access it at a time, from their computer terminal. This reduces the risk of different versions of financial information being available.

This accessibility is one of the key benefits of cloud accounting.

Other benefits include a reduction in paper usage as information can be shared internally, and with customers and suppliers, electronically such as electronic invoicing. Any documents that are received, such as bills, can be scanned into the system for different users to access, rather than photocopying. This **improves sustainability**.

The data on the cloud is encrypted for **security**. However, it is vital that only authorised users have the ability to log onto the cloud to view, use or change that data.

Cloud accounting increases the risk of cyberattacks and the potential loss of, or damage to, data. The cloud provider ensures that the data is encrypted and backed up regularly to minimise the risk.

Users must of course have **access to technology and internet** to be able to access the data on the cloud. Issues with computer devices or connectivity to the internet need to be considered, eg staff working in an area with no mobile signal or WiFi.

3 Artificial intelligence and machine learning

Artificial intelligence (AI): Any computer programme which allows a computer to simulate natural intelligence of humans and perform complex processes.

Accounting systems are processing more and more data. AI can be used to manage that data more efficiently which frees up human time for more complex tasks.

AI can be used for a wide range of tasks such as process automation, forecasting, product recommendations, marketing, chat bots and many more.

3.1 Impact of AI

AI works by learning from past decisions. An AI system could be 'taught' to identify the correct information from a purchase invoice to enter into the accounting system. As well as processing data, AI can also be used to make financial projections based on past performance.

Change in staffing levels

For routine, high-volume transactions, the use of AI can speed up the time take to process information compared to using humans to manually process the data. Machines are also more efficient, and do not require breaks / limited working hours.

Businesses using AI might need less low-skilled staff to process data. AI might also result in senior staff having more time for complex work requiring human judgement as an AI system can also be used to undertake some of the monitoring control work usually required of more senior staff.

Change in error rates

If the AI process has been designed correctly, there are also likely to be significantly fewer errors from AI processed data.

Implementation and running costs

An AI system is only as good as the data that has been put into it. Both the raw data and the AI algorithms need to be accurate for the system to work correctly. Staff also need to be trained to use the AI system correctly. Implementing and AI system will have a significant initial cost which will need to be balanced against the expected future savings from lower staff costs.

Activity 2: Artificial Intelligence

Complete the following sentence:

The ability of a computer system to assist a human operator to make decisions and solve

problems is known as [▼] .

Picklist

- Artificial intelligence
- Data visualisation
- Diagnostic data analytics
- Predictive data analysis

3.2 Machine Learning

> **Machine learning:** The ability of a computer system to learn and adapt by using algorithms to analyse data.
>
> **Algorithm:** A set of rules given to an AI program to assist machine learning.

Machine learning is a sub-set of AI and is when a machine needs to learn from the data it is analysing as part an AI algorithm, in order to continually involve. It involves the machine learning whether its previous analysis was correct and learning from that to improve going forward.

Machine learning can be used to analyse complex data from a variety of sources due to the superior processing speed of a machine compared to humans. Large amounts of data can also be processed very quickly.

However, similarly to AI, there must be human input to create the initial programming/algorithm and then monitor the output.

4 Data analytics

> **KEY TERM**
>
> **Data analytics:** The collection, management and analysis of large sets of data for the purpose of obtaining information that an organisation can use for decision making.

As businesses and their stakeholders use technology, this results in more and more data becoming available. For the data to be useful, it needs to be analysed.

4.1 Types of data analytic

Data analytics can be divided into four categories.

4.1.1 Descriptive analytics

Descriptive analytics are based on live data and tell the user what is happening in real time, eg monthly financial results. This is the most commonly used type of analytics in a business and often takes data from a variety of sources.

4.1.2 Diagnostic analytics

Diagnostic analytics explains why sometime is happening and helps to troubleshoot issues. If management wanted to understand why the monthly financial results were underbudget, then diagnostic analytics could be used to help understand why this had happened. For example, has the sales volume decreased, or have there been fewer customers?

4.1.3 Predictive analytics

One key use of business data is to use it to predict what might happen in the future. Predictive analytics takes historic data from a variety of sources and use that data to make predictions about the future. This could be financial forecasting, or other key metrics like expected number of new customers etc.

4.1.4 Prescriptive analytics

Prescriptive analytics help a business to decide what to do next. AI and machine learning are often used to interpret the data and suggest possible outcomes for a business.

4.2 Impact of data analytics

Data analytics allows a business to make fact-based decisions. Businesses are able to use data analytics to quickly obtain high-quality information from a variety of sources which can be used to inform and justify decisions that are being made.

Data analytics can also be used to identify and correct fraud and errors as unusual data entries can be identified and processed. This might be a customer error, eg ordering 100 items when the usual practice for that customer is to order 10. Fraud can be identified by certain types of data analytics as anomalies or unusual patterns.

Workplace efficiency is another benefit of data analytics. The real time, insightful analysis of data might identify gaps, or improvement areas within an organisation. It can also be used to predict staff levels required in a seasonal business, or inventory levels needed to meet expected demand.

Activity 3: Data analytics

Complete the following sentence:

Data analytics relies on [▼] information.

Picklist

- Confidential
- Digital
- Verbal
- Written

5 Data security

As businesses hold more and more online data, this data needs to be kept secure.

Data security risks include:

- Financial losses from lost business or fines
- Reputational damage
- Operational disruption

It is vital that any business with online data have sufficient security procedures in place to protect that data.

5.1 Risks to data and operations

5.1.1 Cyberattacks

Cyberattacks: Internal or external attempts to access, damage or destroy a computer network or system.

There are a number of different cyberattacks that a business can face. Some of the most common include:

Phishing: Where the cyber attacker sends emails to the victim which appear to be from the legitimate business, asking the victim to divulge sensitive information such as passwords or personal information.

Malware: An abbreviation of malicious software. The cyber attacker attempts to cause damage to the computer or network of the victim. Some of the most common types or malware are viruses, spyware and ransomware.

Ransomware: Ransomware is used to block user access to a device or data until a ransom is paid to the attacker.

Denial of service: The cyber attacker attempts to shut down the network or website of the business. This is often done by overwhelming the system with multiple fake users.

5.1.2 Unauthorised access

Access to data should be controlled. Within an organisation, each staff member should only have access to the sensitive data that they **need** to do their job.

Unauthorised access can also be remote, which is often referred to as hacking. A hacker will attempt to gain unauthorised access to a computer system to stop the system working or to steal data.

5.1.3 Physical loss of equipment

IT equipment which is stored in business premises should be physically secured and password protected.

The increase in mobile technology has resulted in different security requirements, as many business mobile devices have access to sensitive data. These devices should be protected by passwords or biometric data such as fingerprint recognition.

5.1.4 Data issued in error

Data protection laws require businesses to carefully safeguard user data. Businesses can inadvertently user data, eg sharing customer details. There could be significant financial implications for large data breaches.

5.2 Data security measures

As a result of the risks to data, it is crucial for a business to have appropriate data security procedures in place. Data security should protect both the hardware and software that a business has. A business should have a policy of ensuring the best, and most up-to-date security is in place and responsible user agreements for all staff members.

Some common data security measures include:

- Passwords or other access controls – to restrict access to the device or network
- Physical controls – to restrict access to hardware
- Firewalls and internet gateways – to stop data being transmitted into and out of a system
- Malware and virus protection – to identify and stop the installation of unknown and suspicious software

Chapter summary

- Reporting of financial information has been enhanced by the use of data visualisations to aid user accessibility.
- Businesses can also use dashboards to monitor key performance indicators using real time data.
- Cloud accounting has permitted many small or medium sized business to access accounting software for the first time.
- Cloud accounting has many benefits, but there are risks such as loss of data or lack of access.
- Artificial intelligence can be utilised by business to streamline procedures and reduce staff time in performing data processing tasks.
- There are four types of data analytics – descriptive, diagnostic, predictive and prescriptive which can be used to analyse large amounts of data to aid decision making.
- Data security is a key risk for a business using technology. There are internal and external risks to the business and appropriate controls must be put in place to minimise the risk.

Activity answers

Activity 1: Data visualisation

	Picklist
This data visualisation method provides a summary of four or five relevant drivers that give an overview of a business area.	Dashboards
This data visualisation method is often used to show trend analysis.	Line charts

Dashboards are real-time and provide a summary of four or five relevant drivers that give an overview of a business area whereas line charts are used to show trend analysis, or other time-based results (such as sales over the last five years).

Activity 2: Artificial Intelligence

The ability of a computer system to assist a human operator to make decisions and solve

problems is known as | artificial intelligence | .

The ability of a computer system to assist a human operator to make decisions and solve problems is known as **artificial intelligence (AI).**

Activity 3: Data analytics

Data analytics relies on | digital | information.

Information may be written, verbal or confidential, but if it is not digitised it cannot be analysed by data analytics.

Test your learning

1 **Complete the following statement:**

   Dashboard reporting is a [▼] representation of a company's key performance indicators. A dashboard uses [▼] data.

   Picklist
   - Financial
   - Historic
   - Real-time
   - Visual

2 **Identify which of the following statements about cloud accounting software are CORRECT.**

	✓
Cloud accounting software allows users with the correct security details to access the software from any machine in any location.	
One of the disadvantages of cloud accounting software is that many different versions of financial information may be stored as many users can access the same information.	
Use of cloud accounting software decreases the data security risk as the data is stored off site.	
Cloud accounting software has the benefit of reducing paper usage as source documents can be scanned and all financial reports accessed directly from the cloud.	

3 **Identify the category of data analytics in the activities below. Select the option from the picklist (some of the options may be used more than once or not at all.)**

Activities	Category of data analytic
Cash flow forecast for Quarter 1	▼
Monthly sales report	▼
Appraisal of machine purchase with recommendation	▼
Variance analysis for materials	▼

   Picklist
   - Descriptive
   - Diagnostic
   - Predictive
   - Prescriptive

4 **Complete the following statement.**

   [▼] is an example of a data security attack where the attacker impersonates a genuine person or business in an attempt to steal the victim's data.

Picklist

- Denial of service
- Malware
- Phishing
- Virus

5 **Complete the following sentence:**

[▼] allows patterns or trends to be found in data or information where they would previously have been impossible or too time-consuming to identify.

Picklist

- Artificial intelligence
- Cloud accounting
- Data analytics
- Data visualisation
- Machine learning

6 **Complete the following sentence:**

[▼] tools improve the communication of information making it more effective and rich whereas improved consistency of data due to holding and maintaining a single data source shared by multiple users is an advantage of [▼] .

Picklist

- Artificial intelligence
- Cloud accounting
- Data analytics
- Data visualisation
- Machine learning

5 Making changes to systems

Learning outcomes

5.1 Changes to the accounting system

Learners need to understand:

5.1.1 the principle of SWOT (Strengths, Weaknesses, Opportunities, Threats) analysis

5.1.2 how to apply a SWOT analysis to an accounting system

5.1.3 the principles of a PESTLE (Political, Economic, Social, Technological, Legal and Environmental) analysis

5.1.4 how to apply a PESTLE analysis to an accounting system

Learners need to be able to:

5.1.5 undertake a
SWOT analysis

5.1.6 undertake a PESTLE analysis

5.1.7 recommend changes to the accounting system

5.1.8 provide a clear rationale to support recommendations

5.2 Cost and benefit of changes to the accounting system

Learners need to understand:

5.2.1 cost-benefit analysis

Learners need to be able to:

5.2.2 quantify the cost of recommendations, stating assumptions made

5.2.3 review recommendations against ethical and sustainability principles:

- social issues
- corporate issues
- environmental issues

5.2.4 undertake a cost-benefit analysis

5.2.5 recommend changes to the accounting system

5.2.6 provide a clear rationale to support recommendations

5.3 The effects of changes on users of the system

Learners need to understand:

5.3.1 the changes that users may be required to make to working practices to comply with changes to statutory and organisational requirements

5.3.2 that appropriate controls need to be in place during the transition from one system to another

5.3.3 that problems might occur during transition

5.3.4 different methods of support that can be given to users of the accounting system to assist them in adapting to the recommended changes:

- testing
- piloting
- direct changeover
- dual/parallel running
- phased implementation.

Learners need to be able to:

5.3.5 evaluate the implications of changes to operating procedures and time spent

Assessment context

The topics covered in this chapter will be included within a number of tasks in the Internal Accounting Systems and Controls unit assessment.

Qualification context

While this chapter draws on costing principles covered at Levels 2 and 3, for the most part its content is new.

Business context

Management should regularly review the accounting systems for relevance and to ensure that it is working as originally intended. As businesses grow and change, so do the accounting systems within them, therefore management should be ensuring that regular review is undertaken.

Systemic weaknesses in accounting systems require changes to be made, otherwise the system may potentially be exposed to fraud and error. Any system changes need to be thoroughly evaluated to ensure they deliver a value for money solution.

Changes made to the accounting system must be carefully planned and controls put in place to ensure that the business can continue during the time of transition.

 BPP

Chapter overview

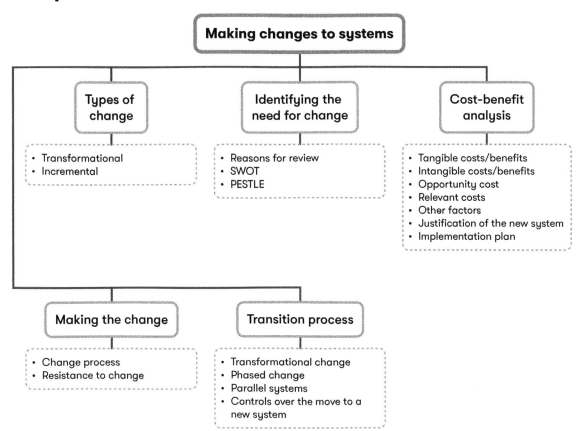

Making changes to systems

Types of change
- Transformational
- Incremental

Identifying the need for change
- Reasons for review
- SWOT
- PESTLE

Cost-benefit analysis
- Tangible costs/benefits
- Intangible costs/benefits
- Opportunity cost
- Relevant costs
- Other factors
- Justification of the new system
- Implementation plan

Making the change
- Change process
- Resistance to change

Transition process
- Transformational change
- Phased change
- Parallel systems
- Controls over the move to a new system

Introduction

This chapter looks at what happens when organisations consider making changes to their accounting system and internal controls.

Before any changes are made, analysis of the existing systems should be carried out to identify what changes are necessary. Either **SWOT** or **PESTLE** can be used to identify changes needed to the accounting system.

To ensure any planned changes generate benefits, the preparation of a **cost benefit analysis** should be undertaken. This helps management identify and understand all of the relevant costs associated with implementing system changes, and the benefits that will be gained from doing so.

Costs and benefits may be **tangible**, meaning that they can be quantified, or **intangible**, meaning they are harder to assess, as they cannot be quantified in monetary terms.

Included in any analysis should be the **opportunity costs** of any actions, eg if money is spent on a new system you should consider where else this could be spent within the organisation (sales promotions or new product development).

Aside from the financial aspects, it will also be important to assess the impact that any proposed changes will have on staff and other stakeholders.

1 Identifying the need for change

In the previous chapters of this Course Book, we have identified situations where change may be needed in an accounting function, an accounting system or a system of internal controls. The need for change can sometimes become apparent when deploying many of the tools we have seen previously, eg fraud matrices, ratios and key performance indicators.

1.1 Reasons for review

Management often have specific reasons to undertake detailed reviews of accounting systems:

Reason	Examples
Personnel changes	Changes in management or departments Department mergers or changes (such as launching a new range of products or diversification) Rapid hiring of staff to meet demand High turnover of staff
Company strategy change	Change in focus for the company strategy Acquisition of a new business (such as in a merger, or takeover) or sale of a business sector
Technology changes	New software or hardware Changes in cyber security (possibly as a result of a cyberattack or the threat of one)
Financial reasons	Management have identified areas requiring cost reduction Development of a new market for the product (such as overseas) Analysis of costs highlighting adverse ratios with similar companies in the same industry

1.2 Timely and regular review

Even if there are no specific reasons to prompt a review of the accounting systems, policies and controls, the systems should still be reviewed on a timely basis.

Often there may be small, incremental changes which are not sufficiently significant to generate a full review of the system, such as a replacement head of department (there is still a supervisor, and the systems are still working as before). However, over time, these small changes may cause an accounting system to be less effective, less efficient or no longer fit for purpose.

Reason	Examples
Changes occurring over time	The system may require additional stages in the process, eg additional authorising staff to cover more purchasing Changes in authorisation levels to reflect current spending Alteration of the holiday approval process to spread 'peak periods' more fairly across staff (no longer first come, first served) Monthly invoice payment runs changed to weekly Weekly paid staff to be paid monthly Moving from cash payments to staff to online banking for salaries and expenses
Post implementation review	Perhaps a new system has been installed but changes are required to improve it. The process of reviewing new systems once they are 'up and running' can elicit further changes
Efficiencies	Efficiencies may be identified which can reduce cost, waste or time: Using online banking instead of cheques E-receipts instead of paper Online ordering process instead of telephone based
Identifying problems before they occur	The current system may be working, but it may be flawed. How does it work in practice compared to how it looks on paper? There may be steps required by overworked line managers which can be shared, automated or changed. If the current system is open to neglect or abuse, then problems may occur. A pre-emptive review of key areas may highlight areas for revision.

2 Types of change

The type of change required can be assessed by analysing:

(a) The **seriousness of the problem** to be resolved – changing a system riddled with inherent weaknesses or subject to fraud is evidently a much bigger job than ensuring an upgrade of an existing off-the-shelf payroll package.

(b) The **scope of the change** – implementing a completely new accounting system is more of a challenge than revising the responsibilities of two members of staff.

(c) The **context** in which change takes place – changes needed to safeguard jobs may be easier to implement than those that staff perceive to be cosmetic in nature, or unnecessary.

The degree of change can be classified as the following:

Transformational change: A wholesale change, eg integrating all accounting functions at a centralised location with a new computer system.

Incremental change: A small change or a big change made in small steps eg gradually moving each sub-system onto an integrated accounting package.

The type of change will depend on what the issues are and how management decide to proceed with the changes. This is covered later in the chapter.

3 SWOT analysis

> **SWOT analysis:** A way for management to highlight the key issues, and review where the organisation has strengths and weaknesses and to consider any opportunities or threats from internal and external sources.

A useful tool for analysing the accounting and internal control system, as part of the **risk assessment process**, is a SWOT analysis. SWOT stands for:

- Strengths
- Weaknesses
- Opportunities
- Threats

The strengths and weaknesses of a system will be **internal** factors.

Once strengths and weaknesses have been identified, recommendations can be made to address the weaknesses.

Opportunities and threats are **external** to the actual system itself.

In these instances, management need to consider how they can use these external opportunities (such as market conditions) or mitigate against potential threats (eg changes in legislation, interest rate changes).

A SWOT analysis is a way for management to highlight the key issues; however, it is important that they focus on only a few at a time as proposing too many changes may be detrimental to staff morale, confusing to customers or clients, or expensive to implement in terms of time and financial outlay.

> **Risk assessment process:** An evaluation of the risks to the achievement of the organisation's objectives.

Activity 1: SWOT analysis

Use the information received in the pre-seen information and Chapter 3 in respect of CCC.

Required

Complete a SWOT analysis for CCC using the format below, focusing on the strengths and weaknesses of the internal accounting systems, and the opportunities and threats for the company as a whole.

Strengths	Weaknesses

Strengths	Weaknesses

Opportunities	Threats

3.1 Limitations of a system of internal controls

The inherent limitations of the effectiveness of internal controls include:

- People make mistakes that may not be picked up by software or human review (**human error**).
- People may not operate controls properly, thus negating them.
- People may deliberately **circumvent** control systems if they want to defraud the company, either individually, or by colluding together.
- Lack of review of the controls in place means that there is no incentive for staff to follow them.
- An overreliance on controls, especially computerised controls, can breed complacency meaning they go undetected.

Assessment focus point

If you are asked in the assessment to consider the limitations of controls, ensure you have read the scenario carefully to ensure your answer is tailored to the question, eg in the case of CCC there appears to be little or no regular review of the controls. Stefan is asked about the aged receivables report when cash flow becomes an issue rather than on a regular, monthly timetable.

4 PESTLE analysis

PESTLE analysis: An approach used for understanding the external factors that affect an organisation (Political, Economic, Social, Technological, Legal, Environmental).

Another model that can be used to identify changes to the accounting and internal control system is the **PESTLE model** which stands for:

- **P**olitical
- **E**conomic
- **S**ocial
- **T**echnological
- **L**egal
- **E**nvironmental

You were introduced to the PESTLE model in the Level 3 unit *Business Awareness*. The categories in a PESTLE model are all external to the company, in the same way as the opportunities and threats are in the SWOT model.

The PESTLE model is a way of categorising these same external factors.

Activity 2: PESTLE analysis

Complete a PESTLE analysis for CCC using the format below. You should categorise the opportunities and threats from Activity 1. You will not necessarily have something in each box.

Political	Economic
Social	**Technological**
Legal	**Environmental**

5 Cost-benefit analysis

A cost-benefit analysis takes recommendations for changes and improvements in the accounting system and its controls and analyses them in terms of the costs and benefits to the company of implementing them.

Change should be cost effective in that the benefits of the change should outweigh its costs.

Both costs and benefits can be tangible and intangible.

> **Cost-benefit analysis:** Analyses recommendations for change in terms of the costs and benefits to the company of implementing them.

A simple **cost-benefit analysis** may look something like this:

	£'000	£'000
Initial costs		
Cost of machinery	500	
Staff training	75	
Site preparation	10	
		585
Annual running costs		
Safety checks (req'd every 2100 hours of production)	150	
Replacement drill heads	14	
		164
Total costs over lifetime (5 years)		749
Savings		
Staff hours savings	25	
Costs of running the old machinery (5 × 155)	775	
		800
Total net benefit over 5 years		51

In order to produce an accurate and meaningful cost-benefit analysis, it is necessary to ensure all costs and benefits are included.

5.1 Tangible costs

> **Tangible costs:** Identified, quantifiable costs of the change eg buying a new software package.

Tangible costs are relatively easy to value as they can be quantified in terms of time and/or money.

Illustration 1: Tangible costs

The tangible costs of a recommended new computer system are the quantifiable cost of:
* The system itself (training, hardware and software)
* The loss of staff time while they are training
* Software licences
* Future upgrades to maintain speed of processing or due to technical updates regarding regulation or other changes

Tangible costs are identified, quantifiable costs of the change eg buying a new software package.

Activity 3: Tangible cost of a new system

CCC has decided to investigate using an accountancy software package called KashCade.

There are three part-time staff in the accounting department, and they are considering adding a full-time member. The directors cannot decide how they will ensure staff are adequately trained. They are also considering whether the warehouse team and the sales team will require system access too. The estimated cost of the sales team being away for a day is expected to be £2,000 in lost sales, with the total cost of using temporary staff in the accounts team whilst they undergo training of £540 (per day).

CCC have used an external consultant (at a cost of £750) who has estimated that the increase in efficiencies will save CCC £6,300 per year. This is in addition to the expected increase in sales (of £5,000 for the first year, increasing by 15% each year) due to the ability to make online sales and reduce inventory holding and tying up cash.

KashCade has broken down the elements of the system as follows:

Dear Sirs,

Thank you for your interest in our integrated accounting system. We are happy to provide you with details of the following:

- Basic System 1 (Cloud) which includes:

- Receivables ledger system, including pre-numbered invoices and aged debt reports

- Payables ledger system, incorporating purchase orders which can be matched against incoming invoices. Inventory aging reports are included.

- General ledger and summary trial balance reports

- Journal functionality

- Exception reporting

- Budget input and comparison tools

- Updates and upgrades occur regularly and will be automated at no extra cost.

Additional add-ons which can be purchased:

- Payroll function which will also integrate with the general ledger and allow full Real Time Information (RTI) to HM Revenue & Customs, as well as year-end reporting and payslip production.

- Draft financial statements reporting

- Advanced inventory option which allocates a FIFO cost and monitors the current inventory cost, allocating costs to allow a 'cost of project' for each customer.

Annual costs

	Initial costs	Annual costs
Basic system 1 (cloud)	£5,000 (to cover assistance with data migration)	£3,250 (up to 10 licensed users)
Payroll	-	£550
Financial accounts	-	£750
Advanced inventory	-	£1,250

We also recommend using our training partner, Best Practical Performance Ltd, to supply the training to staff on the KashCade system.

In-house training (maximum of 15 people) 2 days	£3,500

Course at local college (3 days)	£350 per person
Online course (completed in own time)	£75 per person (license limited to access for 6 months)

We can include a full support system, 24 hours a day by remote operators for £250 per year, with the first year free of charge.

If you have any further questions, please do not hesitate to contact us.

Yours sincerely,

P. Bryan

Sales Director Kash Cade Ltd

Required

Prepare a report showing a brief financial cost-benefit analysis of taking the full page including add-ons, together with additional narrative. Ensure that the following have been included in your report:

(a) Identify the tangible costs of this purchasing decision.

(b) Estimate the overall costs of purchasing this software. Consider also how CCC could reduce these costs, and the implications of doing so.

5.2 Opportunity costs

An **opportunity cost** is the value of an activity that has not taken place, because of a decision to do something else. For example, if a taxi driver is offered a £100 fare for a 2-hour round trip to the airport, they would need to factor in the cost of any regular fares they will lose as a result. If the taxi driver normally makes £30 an hour in regular fares, then the opportunity cost of the airport run is £60, leaving them with an effective benefit of £40 – lower than the £100 fare offered.

Wherever possible, any opportunity costs of making a particular change should be included in the cost-benefit analysis.

5.3 Relevant costs

An organisation may decide that it is more efficient or economical to outsource a service or a department. For example, CCC may decide that it is better to utilise the expertise, albeit at an additional finance cost, in order to run and maintain the payroll and HR function. Refer to *Advanced Management Accounting* if you need to refresh your knowledge on this area.

5.4 Intangible costs

Intangible costs: Cannot be quantified in financial terms, where the costs of the change are more difficult to identify and quantify, eg the cost of lost custom as customers go elsewhere during the disruption caused by the change.

Activity 4: Intangible costs

Consider the new computer system and training programme proposed to CCC in the above activities.

Required

Discuss the intangible costs which may impact the decisions of CCC management on whether to go ahead with the new system, and deciding on which training programme to be undertaken.

5.5 Benefits

There should be at least some tangible and/or intangible benefits of any changes made to the accounting system, otherwise there is no point making them.

> **Tangible benefits:** May be more difficult to quantify than tangible costs, but easy to identify (eg less time spent creating invoices, improved efficiency).
>
> **Intangible benefits:** Benefits of the change that are more difficult to identify and quantify, eg improved reputation for efficiency, improving the customer experience in a showroom, facilitating an increase in the amount of time spent browsing, or making conditions for staff better so that they are more motivated at work.

It may not be possible to put estimated values against every benefit, especially intangible ones, but describing the benefits clearly is extremely important in a cost-benefit analysis. These often form powerful arguments in favour of implementing a recommendation.

A systems change may be due to the availability of a new software package, improving the information which is available to management from the raw data input by the employees. This can increase staff morale, as they are able to work more efficiently or may benefit from the automation of mundane manual tasks. A new system may offer new opportunities for retention of customers or attracting new customers, such as loyalty programmes or bonuses for referring friends to the company.

Activity 5: Benefits of training

Consider again the training discussed in Activity 3.

Required

What intangible benefits might there be in sending CCC's staff on the training programme?

5.6 Other factors to consider

Aside from the costs and benefits already discussed in this chapter, there are other considerations which will impact how an organisation approaches a potential change or assesses whether it is necessary to change or not.

Using a SWOT or PESTLE analysis can help to focus management's attention on the areas that need developing, eg improving customer service or reducing wastage in a manufacturing process.

Where risks have been identified in completing a fraud matrix (Chapter 3), management can use this information to tailor any changes to the system so as to mitigate the most significant risks. This will ensure that changes are focused in the most cost-efficient and effective manner.

Once a decision has been made on the basis of costs, benefits and risks, both from an operational and strategic view, there are further points to consider.

It is vital that any changes made during the transition are 'future proof' as far as possible. For example, any software should be able to cope with new accounting standards or reporting requirements already planned for implementation.

It should also meet the latest regulatory and legal requirements. It is important to ensure that any transitioning or changes to the system or accounting function are carefully controlled and monitored by management, with timely reviews to avoid costly mistakes or hurried remedial action.

5.7 Justification of the new system

Now that we have considered the individual elements of the cost-benefit analysis, it is necessary to present the information in a way which is accessible to the decision makers.

It is essential that a clear rationale is provided to support the requirement for change, and that potential issues have been identified as far as possible, with suggestions for actions to mitigate these risks.

Assessment focus point

Ensure that your recommendations (and highlighted risks) are relevant to the scenario you are given. Use the information provided to keep your answers concise and relevant to the question being asked. Do not ignore recommendations if the question asks for risks and recommendations. Consider your audience: is it the management, owners of the business or the staff?

5.8 Implementation plan

The most important part of the change process will be the detail behind the implementation plan.

This often includes the rationale behind the decision making as well as the main budgetary elements, such as the cost of the consultancy, the costs of new software and computers or other equipment. Contingency costs may be built into the plan, especially where riskier or trickier areas may be taking place, such as extra costs for training, testing of the new system or installation in remote branches of the organisation.

The aim is to give a best view of the main issues and where the costs are to be spent.

The plan should not only cover financial costs, but also consider the morale of staff, including when to inform them of the changes, how often to update them and how this can be best be carried out.

Activity 6: Cost-benefit analysis

Use the information you have been provided with to date, including the answers to the activities in this chapter.

Required

Prepare a detailed cost-benefit report for the two directors which provides an analysis for implementing a centralised, integrated accounting system in CCC, with appropriate staff training.

Assume that the software will initially be used for 5 years.

Where the information regarding the actual cost cannot be defined (due to insufficient available information), show how it may be an issue in the narrative to your report.

(Hint: Think of costs not just in terms of money spent but also in relation to time and any other quantifiable measure.)

Note. Where you cannot quantify either costs or benefits, you should indicate with '£X' within the analysis where a quantified cost or benefit could be determined.

6 Making the change

There are various factors which should be reflected on by management when considering the process for change within an organisation.

6.1 Change process

The main elements of the change process can be described in the following flow chart.

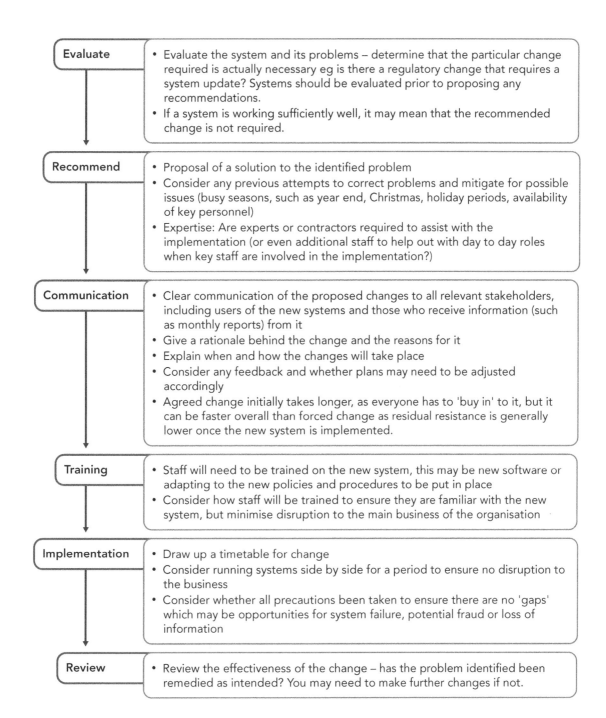

Evaluate
- Evaluate the system and its problems – determine that the particular change required is actually necessary eg is there a regulatory change that requires a system update? Systems should be evaluated prior to proposing any recommendations.
- If a system is working sufficiently well, it may mean that the recommended change is not required.

Recommend
- Proposal of a solution to the identified problem
- Consider any previous attempts to correct problems and mitigate for possible issues (busy seasons, such as year end, Christmas, holiday periods, availability of key personnel)
- Expertise: Are experts or contractors required to assist with the implementation (or even additional staff to help out with day to day roles when key staff are involved in the implementation?)

Communication
- Clear communication of the proposed changes to all relevant stakeholders, including users of the new systems and those who receive information (such as monthly reports) from it
- Give a rationale behind the change and the reasons for it
- Explain when and how the changes will take place
- Consider any feedback and whether plans may need to be adjusted accordingly
- Agreed change initially takes longer, as everyone has to 'buy in' to it, but it can be faster overall than forced change as residual resistance is generally lower once the new system is implemented.

Training
- Staff will need to be trained on the new system, this may be new software or adapting to the new policies and procedures to be put in place
- Consider how staff will be trained to ensure they are familiar with the new system, but minimise disruption to the main business of the organisation

Implementation
- Draw up a timetable for change
- Consider running systems side by side for a period to ensure no disruption to the business
- Consider whether all precautions been taken to ensure there are no 'gaps' which may be opportunities for system failure, potential fraud or loss of information

Review
- Review the effectiveness of the change – has the problem identified been remedied as intended? You may need to make further changes if not.

6.2 Resistance to change

Individuals working within a system tend to put up barriers to change (eg objecting, staging a 'go slow', disputing every detail), even when the change is perfectly valid and even when it is quite small. This is because most people fear change, or rather they fear the uncertainty that surrounds change.

Managers need to be aware of these concerns, and think about how best to overcome the inevitable resistance they will face when planning system changes.

With any proposed and significant change, it is advisable to communicate the reasons and discuss with staff why the change is happening, eg discussions with trade unions, staff representatives, regular updates (email or face-to-face).

Activity 7: Issues during transition

The directors of CCC have decided to investigate how to improve the computer and reporting systems of the accounts team. They are considering the following proposals:

(1) The introduction of an integrated accounting system which will require new training for everyone who uses it, including warehouse staff and sales staff.

(2) Strict reporting deadlines regarding aged receivables reporting and high-level monthly management accounts.

(3) Recruiting a full-time senior qualified accountant to oversee the accounting function.

Required

Identify any problems which may arise at CCC when implementing any of the above proposals.

7 Transition process

> **Transitional process:** Organisations can choose to change in a number of ways including direct changeover (all in one go), phased implementation (a series of changes) and duel or parallel running (operating both old and new systems simultaneously until the old one can be switched off).

Any implementation of a new system or changes to the existing processes should be carefully controlled, including monitoring to ensure there is minimal disruption to normal daily business whilst maintaining sufficient controls to prevent errors or potential fraud.

There need to be strong controls over the implementation of the new system and the transition across from the old one.

7.1 Direct changeover

> **Direct changeover:** A wholesale change from one system to another on a designated date.

As we saw earlier, this is effectively, 'flicking the switch' from one system to another. Without detailed and careful planning, this can result in disarray, however, for smaller, less complex businesses moving from simple systems (such as paper based or simple spreadsheet) this is often the most cost effective method

7.2 Phased implementation

> **Phased implementation:** This uses a series of milestones, with key dates where changes are made.

For some organisations, switching from one system to another in one go is too risky or their systems are too complex to complete in an orderly fashion. For example, the new system may be launched on smaller parts of the business first, such as HR or non-current assets, before moving onto more integrated systems such as purchases and inventory management. Although the process takes longer than the transformational change, it allows a review of the process at each stage, making changes where required to ensure the next process runs more smoothly.

7.3 Dual/Parallel running

> **Dual/Parallel running:** This is where the old and the new system run in parallel with each other.

Dual/Parallel running effectively doubles the workload, eg the staff have to enter the sales orders into two systems instead of one. This does allow an element of 'live testing' so ensuring that the new system can cope with the organisation's requirements, however, it is generally a more costly approach, albeit one which is less risky in terms of lost data, or errors in the system.

7.4 Controls over the move to the new system

New systems are often **tested** prior to using live data, so running a set of test data to ensure that it will provide the reports and the analysis required for the organisation. Sometimes, the system will be **'piloted'** in one area of the business only. This allows management to understand the main benefits and downsides of switching to the new system. Often, only a small group of staff are used to run this piloted system before management decide to proceed with a larger implementation organisation-wide.

Management need to ensure strong controls over the movement of existing data across to the new system. This is discussed at the planning stage to ensure that any consultants are aware of the extent of the data, and the level of required access to it by staff (such as to provide information to prepare financial statements or to support a tax audit). This 'migration of data' to the new system will be carefully managed, and require testing to ensure none is lost in the transition.

Illustration 2: New system

If the management of CCC decide to implement a new accounting system, there needs to be a series of controls regarding the practical aspect of moving the organisation onto the new system.

Management will need to be able to answer a number of questions:

(a) **Existing system** – what will happen to the existing system? Will it be switched off or archived? Maybe it will run 'in parallel' with the new system for a set period of time (this may be tricky as twice the amount of work may have to be undertaken, but it allows for a level of guarantee and security should the new system suffer teething problems).

(b) **Existing data** – how will the existing data be transferred onto the new system? Will it be manually entered or taken across in a 'migration'? How reliable is the old data; will it need cleansing before it is migrated onto the new system?

(c) **Training of staff** – some staff may need to be used in the implementation of the project, so considering who will be trained and when this will happen is important. There may be a need to use temporary staff or external consultants.

(d) **Leadership** – all changes should be monitored, perhaps using a project tool to ensure that milestones are achieved on time, and other issues dealt with as soon as possible.

(e) **Timing** – ensuring that the change is planned in detail, and arranged for a time which best suits CCC

(f) **Security** – how can you ensure that the old system is no longer accessible (either deliberately or inadvertently) by staff? Consider the level of access required for each member of staff on the new system; this may be an opportunity to implement stricter controls and segregation.

 ## Activity 8: Implementation of a new system

Use the information on CCC which you have analysed to date, including the information in earlier chapters.

Required

(1) Consider THREE potential risks and concerns specific to CCC which may cause issues with the implementation of the new system.

(2) Propose any remedial actions which management should consider.

Risks and concerns regarding the new system at CCC	Potential remedial actions

Note. Ensure that the answers are tailored to the needs of CCC using the scenario and other information, eg not just a list of what could go wrong in all scenarios.

Chapter summary

- Change may be needed to an accounting system because it contains systemic weaknesses that make it prone to fraud and error.
- The degree of change necessary depends on: the seriousness of the problem; the scope of the change; and the context in which the change will take place.
- The management of an organisation may well perform a SWOT and/or PESTLE analyse to assess these risks.
- A cost-benefit analysis will enable management to assess the level of change required and whether an alternative option may be preferred.
- To numerically analyse the decision to proceed with a decision (shutdown, make or buy decisions), the relevant costs of a project should be evaluated.
- Costs and benefits may be tangible, such as improved efficiencies, improved customer service or decreased operational costs. These tangible costs can be measured.
- The intangible costs and benefits are harder to quantify, such as improved employee morale due to a better working environment.
- A change may be transformational or incremental.
- The prospect of change can meet with resistance from employees, management, shareholders or customers. It is vital that the expectations and fears of these stakeholders are considered and mitigated in advance of any change occurring.
- Steps for making a change to the accounting system: analyse the system and its problems; choose how to make the change; prepare a plan for making the change; analyse the likely reactions of stakeholders; draw up a timetable for change; communicate the plan and its timetable; make the change; and monitor the effectiveness of the change.
- The transition from one system to another should be planned and controlled to ensure no loss of data and to minimise disruption to the organisation, its employees and customers.
- System changes may be required due to regulatory or legislative changes.

Activity answers

Activity 1: SWOT analysis

Strengths	Weaknesses
• An open plan accounts office ensures that when staff are in and working with each other they can communicate freely and cover each other's work when absent.	• As most accounts staff are part time, there are often occasions when no one is in the office. The door is generally propped open; there is a risk members of the public could access the office.
• The cheque book is kept in a locked desk in the office (but see weaknesses).	• As all staff can access the office and the accounting system with common passwords, there is a lack of control. There will also be issues concerning communication between staff as they are not all in the office at the same time.
• A credit reference agency is used to decide whether to grant credit to new customers.	
• Some credit control procedures are in place.	• Stand-alone computers, with no central system or database, reduce the ability to produce meaningful reports for key stakeholders. There is a risk of loss of data if a computer fails.
• Controls over cheques coming into the office involve a manual day book then accounts.	
• Staff seem keen to improve systems – the Accounts Receivable Clerk has implemented some initiatives.	• Staff as a whole are not qualified in accounting, which poses a risk of errors, exacerbated by the relaxed controls and also a lack of accountability.
• Cash movement is reduced by using cash to make up wages.	• Office staff are paid by cheque – the frequent use of cheques can lead to the risk of cheques being stolen and fraudulently used.
	• Manual calculation of weekly payroll with no secondary check is a weakness as it can lead to errors or fraudulent increases in staff pay.
	• Wages are paid in cash – any use of cash poses a risk of theft.
	• Overdue debts are often not followed up beyond an initial phone call.
	• The cheque book is kept in an easily accessible drawer which is sometimes left unlocked.
	• Staff are not trained in Excel, increasing the risk of errors.
	• Invoices are produced using Word. This has the potential for errors, such as duplication of invoice number or incorrectly calculated.
	• Cash is not counted when removed from the tills on weekdays.
	• No controls over petty cash and over cash taken from tills.
	•

Strengths	Weaknesses
	• No contingency planning – accounting staff are not able to take on each other's roles when absent.
	• No control on authorisation of payments to suppliers – signing of blank cheques to cover absence.
	• Payments to suppliers are made without checking systems or informing other staff.
	• Lack of controls on staff hours may lead to incorrect rotas and staff pay.
	• Pay packets for more than one pay period can be stored onsite. This is a weakness as too much cash is in the office.
	• Unclaimed pay packets left in employee's drawer (risk of theft)

Opportunities	Threats
• There is an opportunity to use one central accounting system on networked computers, which will ensure there is better cover for work when staff are absent and better reporting of key financial information to relevant stakeholders.	• Using spreadsheet software (Excel) to prepare accounts poses a risk of errors being made in formulas that are difficult to spot, resulting in incorrect inventory and accounting information.
• There is an opportunity to train staff in accounting and also in the systems they use, making them much more aware of the controls and procedures they should be operating and also be more efficient.	• The use of one common password is a threat to systems and the data held within them (for example, through unauthorised access).
• There is an opportunity to train staff in each other's roles – perhaps with a backup member of staff for each. This could motivate staff and also ensure cover during absence.	• The lack of formal procedures and controls has contributed to extensive use of the overdraft facility and caused the bank concern. This is a cash flow threat to the company.
• There is an opportunity to re-outsource the payroll function to the company's accountants.	• There appears to be no backup taken of the current systems. This is a threat because key financial data would be lost if the systems failed.
	• Regulatory environment –is constantly changing, for example potential changes to VAT rates. The accounting system needs to be able to recognise these changes and react accordingly.
	• Debt collection – while a relationship with a debt collection agency is in place, this is rarely used due to the costs involved. This may mean that debts are never recovered.

Activity 2: PESTLE analysis

Political	Economic
	• The lack of formal procedures and controls has contributed to extensive use of the overdraft facility and caused the bank concern. This is a cash flow threat to the company.

Social	Technological
	• There is an opportunity to use one central accounting system on networked computers, which will ensure there is better cover for work when staff are absent and better reporting of key financial information to relevant stakeholders. • There is an opportunity to train staff in accounting and also in the systems they use, making them much more aware of the controls and procedures they should be operating and also more efficient. • There is an opportunity to train staff in each other's roles – perhaps with a backup member of staff for each. This could motivate staff and also ensure cover during absence. • There is an opportunity to re-outsource the payroll function to the company's accountants. • Using spreadsheet software (Excel) to prepare accounts poses a risk of errors being made in formulas that are difficult to spot, resulting in incorrect inventory and accounting information. • The use of one common password is a threat to systems and the data held within them (for example through unauthorised access). • There appears to be no backup taken of the current systems. This is a threat because key financial data would be lost if the systems failed.

Legal	Environmental
• Regulatory environment – this is constantly changing, for example potential changes to VAT rates. The accounting system needs to be able to recognise these changes and react accordingly. • Debt collection – while a relationship with a debt collection agency is in place, this is rarely used due to the costs involved. This may mean that debts are never recovered.	

Activity 3: Tangible cost of a new system

(a) The tangible costs associated with the new system might include:

- Initial cost of implementing the new system
- Ongoing annual costs
- Cost of lost staff time for training, if this is quantifiable
- Cost of lost productive staff time, if staff are used to preparing the data for migration to the new system and assisting the software contractors, if this is quantifiable.

(b) Cost of implementing the new system:

Initial costs:	
Basic system 1	£5,000
Training costs ˣ	£3,500
	£8,500
Ongoing annual costs:	
Basic system 1	£3,250
Add-ons	£2,550
	£5,800

These costs would be reduced if CCC decides not to go ahead with all of the add-ons; however, having an integrated system would lead to reduced calculation errors, simpler and faster online reporting (to HM Revenue & Customs for PAYE) and closer monitoring of the inventory chain.

- Initial training costs will be dependent on how many staff will be trained. If at least ten staff members (including both directors) are trained, it would be cost effective to have an in-house training programme. The financial outlay would be the same as sending all ten to college, but it would reduce the travel expenses and would be more likely to tailor the learning experience of the staff.
- The downside would be that ten people would be unavailable to perform business work on the day of training.
- CCC may consider to send selected members of staff to college to complete the learning (eg five staff members costing £350 each; total cost of £1,750) and these staff could act as 'champions' and assist those members of staff who will complete the online training (such as more restricted users, maybe in the warehouse).

The training programme selected will need to be considered in terms of the financial costs, plus the opportunity costs of staff being unavailable to process orders to secure sales.

		£
Basic system 1 – Initial cost		5,000
In-house training	(Most cost effective for 10 members of staff)	3,500
Basic system 1 – Annual cost		3,250

Activity 4: Intangible costs

Intangible costs might include:

- The cost of the 'learning curve' whereby staff will be slower initially on the new software whilst they practise using it. There may initially be teething problems, eg being able to use the reports and understanding what the system can and cannot do.

- Customer dissatisfaction at potential shop closure, or restricted access to staff during the period of transition and training

Activity 5: Benefits of training

Intangible benefits might include:

- Staff are better trained in basic knowledge and skills so they are more efficient.

- Staff morale improves as they feel valued due to the investment in training them, increasing their motivation.

- Customers see well-trained and knowledgeable staff so the company's reputation is enhanced, leading to more repeat custom and recommendations from satisfied customers.

- If everyone is trained at the same time (such as using the in-house training), staff can discuss issues with each other rather than struggling on alone. It will act as a team building exercise and improve morale.

Activity 6: Cost-benefit analysis

A cost-benefit analysis of the recommendation to implement a centralised, integrated accounting system, and to train staff appropriately on it, has been completed as follows:

To: The Directors of CCC Ltd

Date: 23 April 20X3

Cost-benefit analysis on the proposed implementation of the KashCade system and staff training

	£	£
Initial costs		
Initial installation & set up	5,000	
First year's licence £(550 + 3,250 + 750 + 1,250)	5,800	
Training costs (two-day option)	3,500	
Disruption to sales and accounts department (£540 × 2) + sales department (£2,000 × 2)	5,080	
Consultant cost	750	
		20,130
Ongoing costs		
Support system (4 × £250)	1,000	
Annual licence (4 × £5,800)	23,200	
		24,200
Total costs		**44,330**
Savings		
Efficiencies due to new system £6,300 × 5		31,500

	£	£
Increase in revenue/savings due to reduced inventory holding £(5,000 + 5,750 + 6,612 + 7,604 + 8,745)		33,711
Total savings		**65,211**
Total benefit		**20,881**

Costs

Set-up and annual system costs

An example of a system that would suit CCC's needs is a centralised accounting software package, such as KashCade in this example, which has been specifically created for small to medium-sized businesses. There are many similar packages on the market and a full investigation should be completed to determine which best suits the company. A reputable, proven package with a multi-user licence would cost approximately £10,800 (including the initial set-up costs of £5,000 and the first year's licence of £5,800). The basis for choosing the package should include ease of use (eg drop-down menus), the help facility and the user manuals. The ongoing annual cost for licences will be £5,800 per year (£3,250 + £550 + £750 + £1,250), although there may be increases in future years due to inflation or upgrades in the level of cover required by CCC.

Support package costs

CCC would also need to purchase an appropriate support package to ensure users have access to trained support professionals and that software upgrades and bug fixes are received. An estimated cost for this is an additional £250 per year, although KashCade have included the first year free of charge.

Training for staff cost

Appropriate training for staff is required. If the accounting package purchased is one in common use, CCC will be able to purchase places on open courses for staff, costing approximately £350 per staff member. CCC might also consider a tailored training course for all staff at once, to include partial set-up of the system for CCC's use, which would cost approximately £3,500 and staff would be trained over two days minimising disruption to the business. Costs of replacement staff in the accounts department would be £540 per day (totalling £1,080).

There would be an opportunity cost when staff attend the training in that they would not be available to complete their work at CCC while they are on the course. This would be shown as potential lost revenue of £2,000 per day from the sales staff (totalling £4,000).

Hardware and infrastructure cost

The company requires the appropriate equipment to network the computers. This could be completed either by cable or on a secure wireless network and would have a cost. Cabling would be more reliable but would create disruption to the office while being installed, whereas a wireless network would be less disruptive to install but may be less reliable.

A cloud-based system such as KashCade will not require much in the way of installing the actual software, but it is important to verify that the broadband speed and existing computer capacity are compatible with the requirements of the system. There may be an additional requirement to upgrade hardware or to buy new terminals for the warehouse or sales staff. Currently, CCC only has four computers, so more will need to be purchased at a cost for the warehouse and sales staff and directors' access.

Transition costs

CCC would face some disruption while the new accounting system is installed and set up. CCC may need to pay for additional staff time to enter data for customers, suppliers and employees into the system so that it is fully operational, and it is anticipated that this could be completed within one week. This would potentially require an additional week of paid hours.

A further cost the company should consider, but one that is harder to quantify, is staff discontent at a change to the current system. Staff within the accounting team may be unhappy about needing to learn new working practices, increased controls and how to operate a new system. Other employees may see the increased controls in place as preventing them from carrying out their work, and unnecessary.

Procedure manuals cost

There would be a cost associated with producing procedure manuals to ensure staff know the expected working practices and procedures surrounding the new accounting system. There should also be a rota produced for cover when staff are absent. This should be completed by the Senior Accounts Clerk as part of their normal role. As an estimate, this would take approximately 20 hours of their time per year.

Benefits

Increased information benefit

The first benefit to CCC would be the ability to produce reports from the centralised accounting system that provide complete information on the full financial position of the company. These reports can be reviewed on a regular basis by both the directors and the Senior Accounts Clerk. The cash-related reports should help ensure cash flows are effectively managed. This will benefit the company by reducing overdraft fees and avoiding embarrassment with suppliers. The reports produced would include:

- Statement of profit or loss
- Statement of financial position
- Statement of cash flows
- Aged receivable analysis
- Cash flow forecast
- Supplier payment reports
- Costs by cost centre/code
- Analysis of petty cash expenditure
- Payroll reports
- Budgets and budgetary control reports

The financial statements could be prepared in draft format by the accounting team, reducing the input by the external accountancy firm, with a longer-term view to bringing the preparation of the financial statements in-house completely.

Cash flow benefits

An aged receivable analysis can be produced to strengthen the system of chasing overdue debts and ensure customers who have not paid are put on stop quickly. This will prevent customers from taking advantage of the current lax controls.

Cash flow forecasts will enable the directors and the Senior Accounts Clerk to estimate the cash inflows to and outflows from the company, manage cash balances more effectively and reduce the overdraft and related fees. It will also assist with the planning of any significant cash expenditure. Overdraft fees and interest payments could be reduced each year.

Payroll security, accuracy and efficiency

The payroll will be accurately produced when required, with the benefit of the system being up-to-date payroll rules and regulations, such as tax rates. This will produce a benefit of more accuracy, fewer queries and increased efficiency of staff time, as well as compliance with RTI. It is estimated that the system will speed up the completion of the payroll each month. As HM Revenue & Customs (HMRC) requires monthly online payroll reporting, this will ensure that the process is made more efficient as Sonja does not need to type the monthly totals into the system (they will already be there and the software sends the information once it is ready and authorised for transmission).

Disaster recovery

There will be less danger from a system breakdown with appropriate backup of a central system. If one computer were to fail then the other staff could continue working, and a support agreement would ensure that if the main system failed it could be operational again as quickly as possible with less risk of lost or corrupted data. Holding the data in the 'cloud' as KashCade's system does will ensure that upgrades are completed by KashCade rather than a member of the team at CCC having to install the necessary information.

Supplier relations

Another benefit would be improved supplier relations, as suppliers should be paid the correct amounts and on time. This could also benefit the credit terms and conditions that suppliers grant CCC, further improving cash flow.

If the suppliers offer prompt payment (settlement) discounts, these could be monitored and utilised by CCC thus making additional cost savings.

Fraud

Further benefits are the significant reduction in the risk of fraud and the improvement of controls within the system together with improved cost control. Central reports will assist both the owners and the Senior Accounts Clerk with analysing payments and wages, and identifying where costs are higher than expected. Due to current poor controls, it is not known if CCC has suffered from fraudulent activities so benefits are hard to evaluate.

Morale

Another benefit is the improved morale of staff. The accounting team would benefit from training, including formal accounting training as requested, and this would improve their efficiency and effectiveness as well as morale. Better-motivated staff should result in lower staff turnover and also improved commitment to the company.

The morale of the non-accounting staff will be improved by the timely completion of accurate wages.

Regulations

A final benefit is that CCC will be able to comply with regulations such as the Data Protection Regulations with good, secure storage of its data and information. Payroll reporting will be automated and can be completed on time, and VAT returns (if appropriate) can be automatically calculated and sent to HMRC.

Activity 7: Issues during transition

Accounting system introduction

- Training staff, cost and fear of new system especially by some members of the team, such as warehouse staff who may have had limited exposure to computerised inventory systems in the past (the current system is based on Excel)

- Data loss during migration to the new system, or moving data which is incorrect across to the new package. It is important to ensure that data moved onto the new system is correct and accurate. Customer and supplier details should be checked and balances verified. This will take time but it must be completed correctly to avoid issues later on.

Monthly reporting requirements

- Increased pressure on staff at month end may lead initially to resistance to complete the necessary tasks.

- Risk of inaccurate information provided if staff are not trained and motivated to provide quality reports. It is important to explain to staff why this is required, and how it will help the company going forward.

- It is important to establish exactly what the departments need to report on, and where the initial focus will be. It would be a good idea for CCC to focus initially on key areas of

 BPP

weakness, for example cash flow and payments to suppliers, rather than reporting on all variables.

- The current staff has a mixture of accounting experience, with Stefan being a part-qualified accountant. It is important for the directors to ensure that the team are trained and fully understand what information is required. It is likely that CCC will have to invest in staff training in order to make any changes.

Recruitment of a qualified senior accountant

- There could be resistance to the introduction of a new member of management, especially within the accounting team. This may be perceived by existing staff as a criticism of their current performance, breeding resentment and poor co-operation with the new accountant.

Activity 8: Implementation of a new system

Risks and concerns regarding the new system at CCC	Potential remedial actions
Taking into account the time to train up the staff prior to the new system commencing	Review the training plan and consider how the staff will be trained. Discuss options with staff. Consider recruiting temporary staff to cover basic roles whilst the staff are being trained to minimise impact on the day-to-day running of the business.
Choosing a date when the old system will be switched off and the new system will need to be ready and working. When are the busiest times of the year? If customers like to have their new carpet in before Christmas, it may not be a good idea to put in a new system in November, in the middle of the busy season. Do the staff want to start the new financial year on the new system? This may involve last minute work getting the records ready over the Christmas period.	For CCC, given the lack of staff experience and availability, it would be best to plan the system change well in advance to ensure staff are available, and advance notice can be given to customers (and suppliers).
Is the hardware available (computers, printers, broadband speed to the office) sufficient for the new system? Who will be using the system? Just the accounts office, or will warehouse and the directors also have their own terminals? There are currently only four computers so additional hardware may need to be purchased (or upgrades to latest software). If this is a cloud-based system can the broadband cope with several staff members accessing it at the same time – is the broadband speed sufficient or will there be additional costs here too?	Complete a hardware audit, ensuring all computers are accounted for and that their software is up to date and registered by the business (in particular, the computer used in the warehouse may be an issue here). Consider whether additional costs for new or upgraded hardware are to be included in the tangible costs budget for the project. Review the broadband capacity and consider alternatives if required.

Risks and concerns regarding the new system at CCC	Potential remedial actions
Do the systems need to work 'in parallel' so that any errors can be detected early whilst still maintaining a backup system? Consider how the old system(s) will be archived to prevent unauthorised editing access once the new system has gone live.	In a small organisation like CCC, this may be too time consuming and difficult to manage. Propose a hard deadline where the old system is switched off and the new one goes live to minimise confusion with the staff and to reduce inadvertent access to the old system. Ensure the data on the old system is still accessible; however, it cannot be edited.
How will the closing balances from one system be confirmed as correct prior to being set up on the new system and how will the existing data (supplier details, customers etc) be set up on the new system? There may be a resource or skill issue at CCC as the staff work part time and none of them are experienced in changing systems or have sufficient experience to see potential issues.	Cleansing of data prior to migration onto the new system. This will ensure that the new data is accurate – but will take time and staff resources. Once the data is on the new system, management will have comfort in its accuracy. Management may need to consider using expertise brought in from the local accountancy firm to ensure accuracy and the actions are completed prior to migration.

BPP

Test your learning

1   Ard Ltd is a large business with many operating centres. To date, its accounting has been done using various software packages on an independent PC at each operating centre. Ard Ltd now plans to move to a centralised accounting function with an integrated accounting system.

Required

Complete the following statement.

Ard Ltd's plan is [▼] change.

Picklist

- A transformational
- An incremental

2   **Complete the following statement.**

The fact that Ard Ltd's staff in its operating centres will no longer use the skills they have developed in accounting is:

	✓
a tangible cost of the change.	
an intangible benefit of the change.	
a tangible benefit of the change.	
an intangible cost of the change.	

3   **Complete the following statement.**

The fact that Ard Ltd's employees will be disrupted by the planned change, so will not be able to

work on an alternative new project, is an [▼] of the change.

Picklist

- Inevitable consequence
- Intangible benefit
- Opportunity cost

4   In the process of integrating its accounting system, Ard Ltd has discovered some misappropriation of assets and has dismissed the accountant responsible.

Required

Complete the following statement.

This is an example of [▼] change, and ensuring the system is effective following

such a change is likely to take [▼] .

Picklist

- A forced
- An agreed
- Little time

 BPP

- Some time

5 **Complete the following statement.**

Change should be [▼] in that the benefits of the change should outweigh its costs.

Picklist

- Cost effective
- Cost efficient
- Cost neutral

6 There are several situations which may cause an organisation to review their controls and accounting systems.

Required

Using the picklist provided, select the correct answer for each of the following situations

	Reason
A merger of the treasury and the finance function	▼
Management accounts report that the costs for the warehouse department are consistently running above budget	▼
The sales team to be issued with tablet computers to allow them to place orders and check inventory levels, whilst with customers in the showroom	▼
The directors are discontinuing one of the less profitable products, resulting in a refocus on the remaining three core products instead	▼

Picklist

- Company strategy change
- Financial change
- Personnel change
- Technological change

BPP

Test your learning answers

Chapter 1

1 The correct answer is:

	✓
A centralised accounting function has better communication with business units than a decentralised one.	
A decentralised accounting function has more economies of scale compared with a centralised one.	
A centralised accounting function has more economies of scope than a decentralised one.	✓
A decentralised accounting function is better placed to produce group accounts than a centralised one.	

2 The correct answer is:

	✓
Teamwork	
Managers	
Accounting software	✓
Control environment	

Teamwork and managers will have the most significant impact on the culture of the organisation as they will affect how people collaborate, communicate and work together.

The control environment may influence the culture as a stricter or closer monitored set of controls will create a less flexible but more systematic culture.

Accounting software is the least likely to affect the culture as this is a tool used by the organisation. The main impact on the culture of an organisation is how strict any system controls may be.

3 A statement of cash flows shows receipt of a loan as part of   financing activities   and proceeds from the disposal of non-current assets as part of   investing activities   .

4 The correct answers are:

	Ethical ✓	Environmental ✓
Improving recycling rates in the factory by 30% year on year		✓
Changing supplier who can supply the materials 20% cheaper, but with less control over the supply chain	✓	
Installing a carbon capture unit on the main factory costing £2 million		✓
Introducing a more generous pension scheme for employees	✓	

 BPP

All of the decisions will impact the company on a financial or economic basis, either short term or long term (such as the pension scheme commitments and the carbon capture capital installation). It may be argued that treating staff more favourably by allowing them access to a better pension scheme, this would be an ethical decision made by the organisation. Equally, changing the supplier to one whose supply chain may be less transparent could help the profitability of an organisation, but may adversely affect its ethical stance (consider the real life examples where high street fashion chains have sourced their clothing from less reputable companies, and faced a harsh public response as a result). Improving recycling rates and reducing carbon emissions will have an environmental impact as well as a financial one.

5 The correct answers are:

	✓
Fewer direct reports for managers to manager	✓
Clear lines of responsibility	✓
Quicker communication from the top management to the bottom of the organisation	
Reduced costs of management	

A long scalar chain indicates many levels within an organisation, or a tall organisation structure. Quicker communication from top to bottom is an advantage of a flatter structure or shorter scalar chain. There are also likely to be fewer managers in a flat structure, resulting in reduced management costs.

6 Tactical information is used to decide how the resources of the business should be deployed, and to monitor how they are being and have been utilised.

Chapter 2

1

Action	Type of control activity
Person A matches dispatch notes to invoices; Person B creates invoice to customer	Segregation of duties
Control account reconciliation	Arithmetic and accounting control
Petty cash box kept locked	Physical control
Adequate resourcing of accounting function	Organisational control
Review of budgetary control report	Management control

2

Activities	Type of security control
Validation of input data	Integrity control
Passwords	Physical access control
Archiving	System control

 BPP

3 Management should regularly ensure that staff perform $\boxed{\text{reconciliations}}$ of the receivables ledger to ensure accuracy and completeness of the data.

4 Control objectives in relation to taking orders and extending credit are part of the $\boxed{\text{sales}}$ system of the accounting system.

5 Completion of GRNs is a control activity related to the control objective of $\boxed{\text{only accepting goods and services that have been ordered and appropriately authorised}}$.

6 Allocating one customer's payment to another customer's account in order to balance the books and detract from a shortfall is called $\boxed{\text{teeming and lading}}$.

7

Situation	Fraud triangle condition
'They never check on the older items in the warehouse, so they are the easiest ones to steal.'	Opportunity
'I have worked so hard for this company over the years and yet no-one notices. I am definitely entitled to take items out of the stationery cupboard for my own personal use.'	Rationalisation
'If I don't find the money in the next week, my house will be repossessed by the building society. I have to steal cash from the safe because I have no other way of finding the money I owe.'	Pressure

Chapter 3

1

Activities	Type of security control
Batch processing of invoices	Completeness
Only the finance manager can authorise new suppliers on the system	Segregation of duties
Sequential numbering of invoices	Completeness
Alerts to the user when the journal being entered does not balance	Integrity

2 The correct answers are:

	✓
Cost effectiveness	✓
Ease of use	
Reliable	✓
Providing timely information	✓

Ease of use is not a specific objective of an accounting system although it is fair to say that this would be a desirable feature. The accounting system should meet the requirements of the organisation in providing reliable and timely information in a cost-effective manner.

3 The requirement for an accountant to act diligently is part of the fundamental principle of

professional competence and due care .

Professional competence and due care: Having the right level of current professional knowledge and skill to give competent professional service, and **acting diligently** and in accordance with applicable and professional standards.

4 The correct answers are:

	✓
Time	
Responsibility	
Likelihood	✓
Volatility	
Impact	✓

5 The correct answers are:

	✓
Morale	✓
Social	
Reputation	✓
Environmental	
Financial	✓

6 The correct answer is:

	✓
During the analysis of the sales system, a fraud matrix graded the potential loss from misappropriation to be rated 5. Management have decided urgent action is required.	✓
A fraud matrix is a subjective analysis of an organisation's controls, and will ensure that all recommendations identified are actioned immediately.	
A control within the payroll system has been rated as 2 within the fraud matrix. Management have decided that this risk must be rectified immediately.	

A fraud matrix enables the prioritisation of the key risks, focusing on the most significant first. An organisation will then deal with the highest risks first, which is why a fraud matrix grades the risks rather than dealing with all of the weaknesses at the same time.

A fraud matrix rates the lowest risk as 1 and the highest as 5, therefore anything rated 5 should be prioritised over lower rated risks.

Chapter 4

1 Dashboard reporting is a visual representation of a company's key performance indicators. A dashboard uses real-time data.

2 The correct answers are:

	✓
Cloud accounting software allows users with the correct security details to access the software from any machine in any location.	✓
One of the disadvantages of cloud accounting software is that many different versions of financial information may be stored as many users can access the same information.	
Use of cloud accounting software decreases the data security risk as the data is stored off site.	
Cloud accounting software has the benefit of reducing paper usage as source documents can be scanned and all financial reports accessed directly from the cloud.	✓

3

Activities	Category of data analytic
Cash flow forecast for Quarter 1	Predictive
Monthly sales report	Descriptive
Appraisal of machine purchase with recommendation	Prescriptive
Variance analysis for materials	Diagnostic

4 | Phishing | is an example of a data security attack where the attacker impersonates a genuine person or business in an attempt to steal the victim's data.

5 | Data analytics | allows patterns or trends to be found in data or information where they would previously have been impossible or too time-consuming to identify.

6 | Data visualisation | tools improve the communication of information making it more effective and rich whereas improved consistency of data due to holding and maintaining a single data source shared by multiple users is an advantage of | cloud accounting | .
Cloud accounting allows a single data source to be maintained and shared by multiple users.

Chapter 5

1   Ard Ltd's plan is | a transformational | change.

2   The correct answer is:

	✓
a tangible cost of the change.	
an intangible benefit of the change.	
a tangible benefit of the change.	
an intangible cost of the change.	✓

3   The fact that Ard Ltd's employees will be disrupted by the planned change, so will not be able to work on an alternative new project, is an | opportunity cost | of the change.

4   This is an example of | a forced | change, and ensuring the system is effective following such a change is likely to take | some time | .

5   Change should be | cost effective | in that the benefits of the change should outweigh its costs.

6

	Reason
A merger of the treasury and the finance function	Personnel change
Management accounts report that the costs for the warehouse department are consistently running above budget	Financial change
The sales team to be issued with tablet computers to allow them to place orders and check inventory levels, whilst with customers in the showroom	Technological change
The directors are discontinuing one of the less profitable products, resulting in a refocus on the remaining three core products instead	Company strategy change

Scenario

1 Cookridge & Cookridge Carpets Ltd

Company background and history

Cookridge & Cookridge Carpets Ltd (CCC) is a large carpet and flooring dealership based in Southampton, UK. It is the main dealer for 'Umteeko' specialist vinyl flooring in the area and has been trading for four years. It was set up by two brothers, Peter and John Cookridge.

Peter is a trained carpet fitter and has worked in the industry for the past 20 years. Before going into business with his brother, he was the senior manager in a national carpet chain. John was recently made redundant from his role as a mining engineer.

The business was established using John's £80,000 redundancy money and an inheritance the brothers received. Peter managed to raise a loan of £60,000 (using his house as collateral) in 20X2 to refinance the business as the company's bank overdraft was getting large and expensive to maintain.

The brothers purchased a large plot of land on which they developed a building to use as the carpet and flooring showroom. They started out selling and fitting carpets, and then expanded into specialist flooring. This expansion was organised by Peter, who had developed excellent working relationships with carpet and vinyl manufacturers from his time in the industry.

In February 20X1, CCC was asked by Umteeko to become its main dealership for Southampton. Umteeko is a quality product commanding a premium price and requires fitters to have specialist training to fit it.

CCC's mission statement

Our mission is to provide an excellent level of service to all of our customers – and we endeavour to offer our customers a quality product at a competitive price.

We aim to act ethically towards our suppliers, customers and staff, ensuring the best in service and supporting diverse needs and requirements.

The environment is important to us and we aim to recycle wherever possible; we promise to remove all of the packaging from customers' premises and dispose of this in an environmentally friendly way.

Developments in the market

The popularity of Umteeko has grown and, therefore, the supplier insists on reviewing its dealers on a regular basis. All fitters must be fully trained, and qualified fitters are required to attend a refresher course every two years. Umteeko requires that only its specialist adhesives are used in the fitting process to ensure its product guarantees are valid.

Carpets are declining in popularity in the UK market with the rise of allergies, and the difficulties of keeping carpets clean in a busy family home. Wood and laminate flooring, as well as specialist vinyl floors like Umteeko and its main competitor, Kleandarn, are increasing their market share.

The increase in large warehouse-style retailers has reduced smaller retailers' margins on many of the popular brands of carpet and vinyl. CCC is finding it hard to match the prices of the larger retailers on some of the products it is selling.

CCC's strategic planning and control

Strategy mapping

Strategy maps are tools used by organisations to consider how value is created. They evaluate connections between strategic objectives in the form of causes and effects.

Staff

CCC's key personnel are as follows:

Director	John Cookridge
Director	Peter Cookridge
Wages Clerk	Sonja Douglas (part-time)

Senior Accounts Clerk	Margaret Peterson (part-time)
Accounts Receivable Clerk	Stefan Kalinowski (part time)
Showroom and Marketing Manager	Jim Andrews
Warehouse and Operations Manager	Joe Bloggins (joined October 20X2)
Sales staff	Isaac Jackson (sales manager) Ron Sellers Kim Lee
Delivery drivers	Sasha Bilton Lynn Smith
Carpet fitters	Jake Brew Pritpal Iqbal John Smedley David Lee Paul Collins (also can fit vinyl and wood floors)
Vinyl fitters	Sally Burroughs (Umteeko trained) Alan Rogers (Umteeko trained) Jack Brundell

Peter's main hobby is building and racing motorbikes. He is a popular and well-known figure on the local motor-racing scene.

John is married to Paula, who acted as company secretary for the first two years of the company's existence. She then left CCC to train as a solicitor.

The financial statements have been prepared by a local accountancy firm, Bright & Co; however, the directors are planning on bringing the preparation of these within CCC's accounting department. The company does not require an audit.

Extracts from the financial statements of CCC as at 31 December 20X2

Statement of profit or loss for CCC for the year ended 31 December 20X2

	20X2 £000	20X1 £000
Revenue	1,106	930
Cost of sales	(703)	(633)
Gross profit	403	297
Salaries	(312)	(257)
Rent and rates	(30)	(30)
Other costs	(54)	(28)
Profit/loss from operations	7	(18)
Finance costs	(5)	(6)
Profit/loss before tax	2	(24)
Tax	–	–

	20X2 £000	20X1 £000
Profit/loss for the period	2	(24)

Statement of financial position for CCC as at 31 December 20X2

	20X2 £000	20X1 £000
ASSETS		
Non-current assets	78	83
Current assets		
Inventory	85	61
Trade receivables	134	83
Bank and cash on hand	2	4
Total assets	299	231
EQUITY AND LIABILITIES		
Share capital	1	1
Retained earnings	65	63
Total equity	66	64
Non-current liabilities		
Loan	60	–
Current liabilities		
Trade payables	131	86
Bank overdraft	37	78
Accruals and other payables	5	3
Total liabilities	299	231

Extracts from the management accounts for year ending 31 December 20X2

	20X2		20X1	
	Carpets £000	Vinyl £000	Carpets £000	Vinyl £000
Revenue	379	727	425	505
Cost of sales (including materials and staff)	(287)	(416)	(282)	(351)
Gross margin	92	311	143	154
Rent and rates	30		30	

 BPP

	20X2 Carpets £000	20X2 Vinyl £000	20X1 Carpets £000	20X1 Vinyl £000
Salaries: administration and management	87		87	
Salaries: sales	105		60	
Salaries: directors	120		110	
Motor expenses	19		10	
Irrecoverable debts	22		8	
Other costs	18		16	
Total costs		401		321
Net profit/(loss)		2		(24)

Other operational information

The carpet showroom's opening hours are as follows:

- Open six days a week
- Operates from 9:00 am until 9:00 pm, Monday to Saturday

The accounting function works from 9:00 am until 5:30 pm, Monday to Friday.

The accounting function office is located on the first floor of the showroom. Access to the office is by a set of stairs at the rear of the building. Toilet facilities for staff and customers are also on the first floor, so the stairs are used by members of the public.

Once on this floor, access to the accounting function office is easy because the keypad lock is never used – the accounts staff prefer to keep the door propped open. The accounting function office is open plan with no private working areas.

Both the brothers are key holders for the business. They hold the only full sets of keys, as one of them is always on the premises at close of business to ensure the property is secure. There is an alarm code they set every evening when they lock up.

Finance team

The accounting staff use the three computers (using a business version of Microsoft) purchased when the company was set up. In addition, a further two computers were purchased last year which are used by the warehouse team. The warehouse manager used the installation discs from his home computer to put an older version of Microsoft on to save the company some money.

They use spreadsheets for the bookkeeping and payroll calculations (HMRC tax tables are used by Sonja to ensure the correct tax is calculated). Stefan uses a template in Word to produce and print out the sales invoices.

The sales team place orders manually which go to Stefan who raises invoices. Customers are booked in for fitting (if required) or delivery.

Stefan backs up his sales data onto a small, separate hard drive. He has set up similar ones for payroll and purchases but is unsure whether Margaret and Sonja regularly use them. The aged receivables report is compiled by Stefan who enters the invoices onto an Excel spreadsheet. Any unpaid invoices which are over 35 days late are sent to a debt collection agency.

The finance team prepare quarterly management accounts, and these are given to management by the 20th of the month following the quarter end. The management accounts include a basic summary of the revenue and costs for the period, a budget control report and any other information requested by the management team; sometimes it is the aged receivables ledger and sometimes it is a review of the payroll costs.

Margaret is responsible for the company cheque book and keeps it in a drawer at her desk.

Fitting team

The delivery dates are set up by the sales team and discussed with the operations manager.

The fitters are then given a set amount of time to fit the flooring based on the product they are fitting; however, not all of the fitters work to the same standard and some are quicker than others. Some of the Umteeko fitters complain that there is not enough time to follow the full procedures required of the product.

Glossary

Chapter 1: The accounting function

Centralised accounting function: All accounting tasks are performed at head office, regardless of where the company's other activities are carried out.

Corporate social responsibility reports: Outline the objectives for ensuring the ethical, sustainable and moral aims and achievements of the organisation.

Culture: This is 'the way we do things around here'. It may be very different from the way a company might ideally want it to be.

Decentralised accounting function: Data is stored and processed locally, and perhaps independently by staff at different locations or with different computer networks.

External stakeholders: This group of stakeholders includes customers, suppliers, banks and public groups.

Financial accounting: Producing financial statements and other external reports for regulators, including taxation, about the position and performance of the company for a certain time period.

Internal stakeholders: This category of stakeholders includes employees, management and owners (eg shareholders).

Management Information System (MIS): The processing of the various information using computers and computer software from multiple departments or functions.

Management Information: Information provided to management to help them with planning, controlling, performance measurement and decision making.

Management accounting: Provides managers with financial information that they can use in order to make critical decisions that affect how the company is run.

Mission statement: A statement of a company's main objective, and its purpose, strategy and values.

Operational information: Used to ensure that specific tasks are planned and carried out properly within a factory or office. The operational level would deal with cash receipts and payments, bank reconciliations and so forth.

Outsourcing: Where an organisation arranges for essential, but often routine or specialised, tasks to be carried out by a third party.

Stakeholder: Individuals or groups that, potentially, have an interest in what the company does.

Statement of cash flows: An analysis of how and why the company's cash balance has changed during a reporting period. In addition to the statement of financial position and the statement of profit or loss, it is important for both management and current and potential investors to understand how cash is being utilised by the business.

Statement of changes in equity: A reconciliation of the opening and closing equity balances for the reporting period. It enables stakeholders to see the impact of new share issues, profit or loss for the period and dividends paid to equity shareholders.

Statement of financial position: A list of all of the assets, liabilities and equity of the business at a particular point in time (the end of the reporting period).

Statement of profit or loss: A summary of the activity of the company during the reporting period (usually a year).

Strategic information: Used to (a) plan the objectives of the company and (b) assess whether the objectives are being met in practice.

Tactical information: Used to decide how the resources of the business should be deployed, and to monitor how efficiently they are being used. The tactical level would deal with cash flow forecasts and working capital management.

Transaction processing: Maintaining the accounting records: payroll, receivables ledger, payables ledger, cash book and general ledger.

Treasury management: Managing the organisation's cash flow and requirements for finance.

Chapter 2: Internal control systems

Accounting controls: Controls which help to identify mistakes in the accounting records.

Authorisation and approval of transactions: Undertaken by supervisors and managers – this shows the person processing the transaction that it is valid, eg overtime should be approved by departmental heads.

Authorisation controls: These ensure that only authorised personnel can make changes, such as to standing data or to authorise a bank payment.

Confidentiality: Not disclosing confidential information except in appropriate circumstances, and not profiting from confidential information.

Control activities: Policies and procedures that help ensure that objectives are carried out.

Control environment: Formed by the attitudes, awareness and actions of management and those responsible for ensuring that the internal controls within the company meet that company's needs.

Ethical values: Assumptions and beliefs about what constitutes 'right' and 'wrong' behaviour.

Ethics: A set of generally accepted principles that guide behaviour.

Fraud controls: Internal controls specifically against fraud in the areas of staff controls, management controls, physical controls and IT controls.

Fraud: A crime in which the criminal **intentionally** makes a gain or causes a loss to another person by depriving them of assets.

Fundamental principles of professional ethics: The principles that underpin how a professional accountant should behave.

Information processing controls: Controls relating to the transactions and standing data in the computerised accounting system.

Integrity controls: To verify and validate input data, the processing of data and the production of reports.

Integrity of data: Ensures that data is complete, secure and accurate.

Integrity: Being straightforward and honest in all professional and business relationships.

Internal controls: Policies and procedures that address the risk that the aims and objectives of the company will not be met.

Misappropriation of assets: Theft, teeming and lading, payment of false employees or suppliers.

Misstatement of the financial statements: The overstatement of assets or profit, or the understatement of profit, losses or liabilities.

Objectivity: Not allowing bias, conflict of interest or undue influence of others to override professional or business relationships.

Physical controls: Ensure assets such as inventory and cash are safe.

Physical controls: Ensuring assets such as inventory and cash are safe.

Processing controls: May be used to warn the user if they try to log out before processing is finished or close a document prior to saving. Data is also checked for arithmetical accuracy.

Professional behaviour: Complying with relevant laws and regulations and not bringing disrepute on the accounting profession.

(AAT, 2017)

Professional competence and due care: Having the right level of current professional knowledge and skill to give competent professional service, and acting diligently and in accordance with applicable and professional standards.

Reconciliations: Checks where staff ensure that two different sources of information agree or that any differences are understood, eg bank reconciliations verifying the bank statement to the bank account on the nominal ledger.

Reviews: Performed by supervisors or managers by looking at summaries and reports of transactions, eg to ensure they are reasonable.

Security controls: Controls in the accounting system that cover integrity controls, system controls and physical access controls.

Segregation of duties: Making sure that a number of people are involved in different parts of each process to minimise the opportunity for fraud and error.

System of internal control: The control environment, the entity's risk assessment process, the entity's processes to monitor the system of internal control, the information system and communication and control activities.

Systemic weaknesses: Weaknesses that arise within the accounting system itself, which leave it open to fraud and error.

Chapter 3: Accounting systems

Accounting system: A system that takes raw data on transactions as its input, processes this, and then produces many outputs to meet the information needs of stakeholders.

Authorisation of transactions: This is a key control activity, indicating to accounting staff that the transaction in question is valid.

Cost effectiveness: This ensures that something is good value.

Fraud matrix: A map of the potential frauds against an organisation, cross-referenced to the risks of each of these occurring, documenting the controls over these risks. Also known as a risk matrix.

Monitoring, review and report: In this context, **monitoring** means looking at activity or behaviour related to a specified fraud risk because you need to know the extent of this activity or behaviour.

Review means gathering evidence of this activity or behaviour to understand the extent of this fraud risk.

Report means what you communicate to those higher up in the organisation as part of the overall risk management process.

Reliability: This ensures a process or system performs consistently well.

Risk assessment process: This includes the following: identify the risk; evaluate the risk; respond to the risk (manage/mitigate risk by taking appropriate action); ensure compliance (legal and regulatory); monitor, review and report.

Risk of fraud: The likelihood of the fraud occurring and its impact if it does occur.

Risk: The threat to the company presented by the control objective not being attained.

System flowchart: A diagram that shows the flow of the accounting system using boxes and text to show the logic.

Timeliness: This means that the system should provide information at the required time.

User manual: An accurate analysis of how the accounting system and its controls operate, and how they should be used.

Chapter 4: Impact of technology

Algorithm: A set of rules given to an AI program to assist machine learning.

Artificial intelligence (AI): Any computer programme which allows a computer to simulate natural intelligence of humans and perform complex processes.

Cloud accounting: Allows users to remotely access the accountancy software from any location or computer.

Cyberattacks: Internal or external attempts to access, damage or destroy a computer network or system.

Dashboard reporting: A visual representation of a company's key performance indicators (KPIs) using data visualisations.

Dashboard: Uses real time data from the company's accounting and other systems to give an accessible overview of the company's performance.

Data analytics: The collection, management and analysis of large sets of data for the purpose of obtaining information that an organisation can use for decision making.

Data visualisation: The representation of information in the form of a graph, picture, chart etc which will allow the user to see the patterns and outliers in a data set.

Denial of service: The cyber attacker attempts to shut down the network or website of the business. This is often done by overwhelming the system with multiple fake users.

Key performance indicator: The metric or information needed by management to assess the performance of a part, or all, of the business.

Machine learning: The ability of a computer system to learn and adapt by using algorithms to analyse data.

Malware: An abbreviation of malicious software. The cyber attacker attempts to cause damage to the computer or network of the victim. Some of the most common types or malware are viruses, spyware and ransomware.

Phishing: Where the cyber attacker sends emails to the victim which appear to be from the legitimate business, asking the victim to divulge sensitive information such as passwords or personal information.

Ransomware: Ransomware is used to block user access to a device or data until a ransom is paid to the attacker.

Chapter 5: Making changes to systems

Cost-benefit analysis: Analyses recommendations for change in terms of the costs and benefits to the company of implementing them.

Direct changeover: A wholesale change from one system to another on a designated date.

Dual/Parallel running: This is where the old and the new system run in parallel with each other.

Incremental change: A small change or a big change made in small steps eg gradually moving each sub-system onto an integrated accounting package.

Intangible benefits: Benefits of the change that are more difficult to identify and quantify, eg improved reputation for efficiency, improving the customer experience in a showroom, facilitating an increase in the amount of time spent browsing, or making conditions for staff better so that they are more motivated at work.

Intangible costs: Cannot be quantified in financial terms, where the costs of the change are more difficult to identify and quantify, eg the cost of lost custom as customers go elsewhere during the disruption caused by the change.

PESTLE analysis: An approach used for understanding the external factors that affect an organisation (Political, Economic, Social, Technological, Legal, Environmental).

Phased implementation: This uses a series of milestones, with key dates where changes are made.

Risk assessment process: An evaluation of the risks to the achievement of the organisation's objectives.

SWOT analysis: A way for management to highlight the key issues, and review where the organisation has strengths and weaknesses and to consider any opportunities or threats from internal and external sources.

Tangible benefits: May be more difficult to quantify than tangible costs, but easy to identify (eg less time spent creating invoices, improved efficiency).

Tangible costs: Identified, quantifiable costs of the change eg buying a new software package.

Transformational change: A wholesale change, eg integrating all accounting functions at a centralised location with a new computer system.

Transitional process: Organisations can choose to change in a number of ways including direct changeover (all in one go), phased implementation (a series of changes) and duel or parallel running (operating both old and new systems simultaneously until the old one can be switched off).

Bibliography

AAT (2016), *Accounting for good* (2016) [Online] Available from: https://www.aat.org.uk/prod/s3fs-public/assets/Accounting-for-good-report-FINAL.pdf [Accessed 21 March 2024]

AAT (2017) *Code of Professional Ethics.* [Online]. Available from: https://www.aat.org.uk/prod/s3fs-public/assets/AAT-Code-Professional-Ethics.pdf [Accessed 21 March 2024].

AAT (2019) *Could you spot these 5 signs of financial crime?* (article from AAT magazine Nov/Dec 2019) [Online] Available from: https://www.aatcomment.org.uk/aatpowerup/ethics-info/could-you-spot-these-5-signs-of-financial-crime/ [Accessed 21 March 2024]

Cressey, D.R. (1973) *Other People's Money.* New Jersey, Montclair: Patterson Smith.

Datapine cash management example dashboard [Online] Available from: https://www.datapine.com/dashboard-examples-and-templates/finance [Accessed 21 March 2024]

Financial Conduct Authority (2019) *FCA fines Standard Chartered Bank £102.2 million for poor AML controls.* [Online]. Available from: https://www.fca.org.uk/news/press-releases/fca-fines-standard-chartered-bank-102-2-million-poor-aml-controls [Accessed 21 March 2024].

Jaguar Land Rover (2020) *Responsibility.* [Online]. Available from: https://media.jlrms.com/2021-07-19/pdf/ec889077-c450-4849-99f9-791e35eb65b4/Annual%20Report_compressed.pdf?VersionId=XQ_UeGywZN8eq21ZzQk.rUVy7SSITrAv [Accessed 21 March 2024].

John Lewis Partnership PLC, *Annual Report and Accounts 2021* (2021) [Online] Available from: https://www.johnlewispartnership.co.uk/content/dam/cws/pdfs/Juniper/ARA-2021/2021-Annual-Report-and-Accounts-Report.pdf [Accessed 21 March 2024]

Reuters (2017) *Tesco to pay £214m to settle false accounting charges* [Online]. Available from: https://www.reuters.com/article/uk-britain-tesco-fraud-idUKKBN16Z0KD [Accessed 21 March 2024]

Serious Fraud Office (2017) *SFO completes £497.25m Deferred Prosecution Agreement with Rolls-Royce PLC.* [Online]. Available from: www.sfo.gov.uk/cases/rolls-royce-plc [Accessed 21 March 2024].

BPP

Index

Tell us what you think

Got comments or feedback on this book? Let us know.
Use your QR code reader:

Or, visit:
https://www.smartsurvey.co.uk/s/W30E6Y/

Need to get in touch with customer service?

www.bpp.com/request-support

Spotted an error?

https://learningmedia.bpp.com/pages/errata

Tell us what you think

Add comments or feedback on this book. Let us know. Use your QR code reader.

Or visit

https://www.smarturl.org.uk/sW3DFbX

Also log in touch with customer services

Stocked on world

https://www.smarturl.org.uk/customer-services